D0457479

How to Save
Your Kids from Ruin

...

What others are saying about
How to Save Your Kids From Ruin:

"Jerry Johnston is one of the most gifted, effective youth workers of our time. Young people are experiencing one of the most dangerous times in history to grow up. Jerry's keen insights will help parents understand and love their children more, and with God's help, inspire themto a life of true happiness and fulfillment."

Dr. Bill Bright
President, Campus Crusade
for Christ International

"How to Save Your Kids From Ruin *comes out of a rich experience with families of every color, race, and culture. Jerry Johnston knows the family. He cares for the kids. He has the answers."*

Torrey M. Johnson
Carol Stream, IL

"Jerry Johnston loves kids—and families. How to Save Your Kids From Ruin *reflects his devotion, his passion, to make an impact on our troubled world. My wife and I would certainly have appreciated such a valuable resource when we were young parents. Yet even now, those of us with grown children can make improvements. It's never too late."*

Dr. James P. Gills, M.D.
Tarpon Springs, FL

"Many young people today are restless, confused, lonely, and misunderstood. The lack of a loving family relationship and instruction in biblical values and morals is very often the cause of their dilemma. Jerry Johnston addresses this issue with insight, compassion, and understanding. Every parent will benefit from reading this book."

Frank Reimer
Winnipeg, MB, Canada

HOW TO SAVE YOUR KIDS FROM RUIN

Jerry Johnston

VICTOR BOOKS
A DIVISION OF SCRIPTURE PRESS PUBLICATIONS INC.
USA CANADA ENGLAND

All Scripture references are from *The Living Bible,*
© 1971, Tyndale House Publishers, Wheaton, IL 60189.
Used by permission.

Copyediting: Jerry Yamamoto; Barbara Williams
Cover Design: Russ Peterson

Library of Congress Cataloging-in-Publication Data

Johnston, Jerry, 1959–
    How to save your kids from ruin / Jerry Johnston
        p.   cm.
    Includes bibliographical references.
    1. Parent and teenager. I. Title
    HQ799.15.J64   1994
649'.125–dc20   94-26471
                                                        CIP

. . .

To my cherished Aunt Sara.

*You were a surrogate parent to
me during one of my neediest moments.
Because of you, I was spared from
ruin. I will always be grateful.*

. . .

Contents

Foreword ... 9

Preface ... 11

Acknowledgments ... 13

14 Commandments For Parents ... 15

1   I've Been a Good Parent, I Think ... 17

2   Wake Up, Mom and Dad ... 27
Step #1—Don't Be Naive!

3   Where Are June, Ward, and the Beaver? ... 35
Step #2—Be Informed!

4   Do You Have an Ear? ... 47
Step #3—Start Listening!

5   I Don't Want to Go Swimming ... 57
Step #4—Be Discerning!

6   I'm Dying to Talk with You ... 71
Step #5—Start Talking!

7   Three Squeezes Means... ... 87
Step #6—Embrace Them!

8   Follow Me...You'll Be OK ... 93
Step #7—Model the Message!

9   We Care, Amy ... 101
Step #8—Care Enough to Correct!

10   I've Got a Dream   . . . 113
Step #9—Nurture the Dream!

11   I'm Ready, I've Got an Answer   . . . 125
*Step #10—Teach Prepared Reaction
Responses!*

12   You're the Greatest!   . . . 133
Step #11—Instill Super Self-value!

13   I Wasn't Able to Handle the Pressure   . . . 153
Step #12—Enforce "Just Say Wait!"

14   It's a Violent Home   . . . 167
*Step #13—Protect Them—Virtue,
Not Violence, in Your Home!*

15   Teach Me How, Aunt Sara   . . . 177
Step #14—Pray with Them!

Recommended Reading   . . . 189

Foreword

*I*n this time of troubled families, it is comforting to know that someone is writing a book to help parents deal more effectively with their children. Jerry Johnston is that person! Jerry gives parents insight into the world of teens.

This book is packed with insights and helpful hints on how to keep your kids straight in this ever-changing and hostile world.

You will read stories about teens who have murdered and committed other crimes. Letters from suicidal teens who have written to Jerry for help are also included in this book. The teens have become overwhelmed with the problems of this world and feel that they cannot turn to their parents for help so they have written to Jerry as a final act of desperation.

There are also letters from parents who are having problems dealing with their teens. These parents have written to Jerry for guidance in the struggle to raise good teens in a world where it is so easy for teens to fall through the cracks.

There are so many problems bombarding our kids every day that unless we teach them how to face them they will be forever ruined. This book faces those problems and teaches parents and kids to lean upon God for strength.

Also included in this book are stories about raising kids from all aspects of life. Some of the parents are famous and some are parents just like you and me. All of the parents, whether famous or not, have stories to help all of us in raising our kids to be Christians.

This book is a MUST for all parents!

—Josh McDowell

Preface

A Minneapolis invitation to speak came to me with this request: "Tell us how to reach our kids. Tell us how to save our kids from ruin." Here was a specific invitation not only to speak but also exactly what topic to address.

In my preparation, I began to think of the hundreds of young people I had counseled who reflected poor parenting. For years, I have received unusual letters from teens and parents which revealed the severe problems they have gone through.

I put together a message entitled, **"How to Save Your Kids from Ruin."** The response was overwhelming in Minneapolis. Soon I began to share this same message in many other cities from Anchorage, Alaska to West Palm Beach, Florida. Everywhere I went, parents came to me afterward and said, "We really needed that. Thank you so much."

It was apparent that parents were begging for sensible help in reaching and saving their own children from disaster, and they responded and cried for more information. Consequently, this book was born.

Instead of boring you with just a series of outlines on various parenting themes, I have purposely written this book with true stories that illustrate its principles. Each story demands your undivided attention. I only hope you will read and reread each one of them.

I found that a "life" reaches a "life." These wonderful people who have participated by sharing their personal story and pain in *How to Save Your Kids from Ruin* will reach your family and your children.

I recommend that husbands and wives read this book together. After you have done that, give it to your children and ask them to read it also. This book is designed for every member of the family to read. (My own teenage daughter, Danielle, read it and reminded me of some things I wasn't doing!)

My personal goal is to be the best dad I can possibly be. I hope someday to be able to rest in the fact that my kids did not have to go through the trauma I experienced. Far more than that, I want them to experience the greatest happiness in life possible by making the *right* decisions as they grow up. I know you desire that for your children as well. This book will help you reach those goals.

If this book touches you like it did me, recommend it to a parent or an aunt, uncle or grandparent who may be serving as a surrogate parent. Together, we *can* make a difference and save many young lives from ruin.

Jerry Johnston
Kansas City

Acknowledgments

*T*o accommodate writing a book in my already over- whelming schedule is not an easy assignment. It truly required a team effort to complete this volume.

To Danielle, Jeremy, and Jenilee, I express my deep grati- tude. They kept the house quiet and patiently waited for me to play another game of basketball. (I whipped them every time.) My kids bring me down to earth and constantly remind me of the things that are really important. I love you.

Christie, my wife and closest friend in life, helped me cull out the most appropriate anecdotes to use to illustrate the principles of this book. It was not an easy assignment. We were up late and back at it early the next morning. Through it all, I believe it has made us better, more sensitive parents. We have seen anew the incredible responsibility God has given us in parenting.

Dolores Cole, my scheduling associate, helped me in many different ways. She has served faithfully at my side for years, and I have always admired her unwavering faith.

Carolyn Debiak spent many hours proofreading. I couldn't have done it without you.

Thousands of people all across America proved to me this book was desperately needed. When it began in the form of a spoken message, I knew I had hit a deep need. Conse- quently, this book was born. Moms and dads everywhere demanded that it be written.

Finally, to the parents who worked with me and shared their painful experiences, I am most appreciative.

. . .

"Pain insists upon being attended to. God whispers to us in our pleasures, speaks in our conscience, but shouts in our pains: it is His megaphone to rouse a deaf world."

—C.S. Lewis

. . .

14 Commandments
For Parents

1. *Don't Be Naive!*
2. *Be Informed!*
3. *Start Listening!*
4. *Be Discerning!*
5. *Start Talking!*
6. *Embrace Them!*
7. *Model the Message!*
8. *Care Enough to Correct!*
9. *Nurture the Dream!*
10. *Teach Prepared Reaction Responses!*
11. *Instill Super Self-value!*
12. *Enforce "Just Say Wait!"*
13. *Protect Them — Virtue, Not Violence, in Your Home!*
14. *Pray with Them!*

Please post this in a place in your home where you will see it and refer to it often.

. . .

Chapter 1

. . .

I've Been a Good Parent,
I Think

"I've been as good a parent as I could possibly be, I think. We've been a very close family. We've done everything you do according to the book—taken vacations together, gone on backpack trips together, traveled extensively all over the world. We've been a good Christian family. My wife and I tried to set a good example by *being* a good example. We have tried to keep our children up to date on what dangerous things are, but perhaps we did not bear down as hard as we should."

In 1969, Art Linkletter, who uttered these words, had recorded a popular song with his youngest daughter, Diane, entitled, "We Love You—Call Collect." A few months later, Diane, age 20, took a hit of acid and, with her boyfriend trying to grab the belt loops of her dress, jumped to her death out of the kitchen window of her sixth-floor Hollywood apartment. It was a supreme tragedy that stunned her parents and the nation.

Art and Lois Linkletter were good parents. Nevertheless, they experienced a surprising turn of events down "Parenting Lane," which every dad and mom fears might happen. The Linkletters are not alone in their heartache.

Karl Marx's two daughters, Laura and Eleanor, both committed suicide. Eleanor, the youngest, wore her nicest white dress the day she drank poison to end her troubled life.

Paul Newman's son, Scott, overdosed on drugs and alcohol. Gregory Peck's oldest son, Jonathan, was found dead in his apartment, where he had shot himself in the head. J. Paul Getty's son, George, heir intended to carry on the oil company fortune, died of a drug overdose.

Thomas Alva Edison, with just four years of formal education, transformed the world. He invented the light bulb, the phonograph, a vote recorder, a stock exchange ticker, and the motion picture player. These were just 5 of his 1,093 patents!

"Genius is 1 percent inspiration and 99 percent perspiration" was his motto, and he spent endless hours on his inventions. Edison spent so much energy in his laboratory that he had little time for and paid ineffectual attention to his six children. Thomas, Jr., his son, wrote to his dad, "I don't believe I will ever be able to talk with you the way I would like to because you are so far my superior in every way that when I am in your presence, I am perfectly helpless."

In 1935, four years after the death of his ingenious, renowned father, Thomas, Jr., who had drinking problems, committed suicide.

Albert Einstein, who wrote *The Theory of Relativity* in 1905 and won the Nobel Prize in 1921, had a son by the name of Hans Albert. In a letter, Hans reflected on the relationship with his father. "Probably the only project he ever gave up on was me! He tried to give me advice, but he soon discovered that I was too stubborn and that he was just wasting his time."

Einstein's other son, Eduard, suffered a nervous breakdown in 1929. Eduard was also diagnosed schizophrenic, and extensive psychiatric treatment did not seem to help. In the end, he was institutionalized.

Oddly, on the other hand, Al "Scarface" Capone, one of the most murderous gangsters of the 1920s, who died of syphilis in 1947, had a son by the name of Albert. Albert quit his job as a used car salesperson just because the boss was turning back some of the odometers of the cars on the lot.

Albert thought it was dishonest. Later, Albert moved to Florida and changed his name to Albert Francis and stated he wanted nothing to do with the Capone name.

Of Winston Churchill's four children, none developed into his prominence. Three led very troubled lives. Churchill's oldest daughter, Diana, committed suicide in 1963. Randolph, his son, suffered from cirrhosis of the liver, which was caused by heavy drinking. The great leader of England was deeply troubled by his own children.

Strangely, of Madalyn Murray O'Hair's two sons, one is an atheist administrating her operation in Austin, Texas, and one is an evangelical Christian. My friend, Bill Murray, was used by his mom as the fourteen-year-old plaintiff to eject Bible reading and prayer out of U.S. public schools in the landmark 1963 Supreme Court case.

At one time, Bill was an atheist. He later revealed that such a concentration of hate proved to him there must be a God. Since his change, his mother won't speak to him.

Billy Sunday spoke to over 100 million people in person from 1908 to 1920. He reached hundreds of thousands with his fiery message. Yet Sunday could not reach his own sons. One of them, George, divorced his first wife, Henrietta, leaving their two boys behind. Billy Jr., his other son, frequented the speakeasies, consumed illegal drinks, and danced the nights away, all the while embarrassing his famous father because he was the piano player for the evangelistic team.

Because of the infidelities of Sunday's sons, their ex-wives threatened to make the matter public unless Billy Sunday paid them off. With lawyers handling the arbitration on amounts ranging from $5,000 to $36,000, each plaintiff settled out of court, keeping the scandals somewhat quiet.

History makes it quite clear that one of Billy Sunday's greatest hindrances was his children. It seems only his daughter, Helen, was a blessing to her parents. Sadly, she died of pneumonia at age forty-two. George, after a series of wrong decisions, ultimately committed suicide. Of the 1 million respondents to Billy Sunday's powerful invitations,

George was not one of them.

Of TV minister Oral Roberts' four children, Rebecca, Ronnie, Richard, and Roberta, it is Ronnie that few know anything about. As a youngster, Ronnie knew thirty Gospel choruses by heart. He was an outstanding student, fluent in five languages. He represented his high school as a foreign exchange student to Bonn, Germany.

Ronnie enrolled at Stanford University, unbeknownst to Oral that this was the onset of a very troubled future. Evelyn, Oral's wife, always felt and openly admitted that Oral and she were partly to blame for Ronnie's demise. Did it put too much pressure on him to be accepted at Stanford? Oral and Evelyn encouraged the move because they were very proud to have a child smart enough to attend Stanford. Retrospectively, they have repeatedly questioned their motives.

After his freshman year, Ronnie began questioning his father on the biblical truths on which he was raised. This took its toll on Ronnie, and in his sophomore year, he dropped out and joined the army. Later, he married Carol, a beautiful girl, and they had two children, Rachel and Damon. Tragically, however, his marriage collapsed, and Ronnie spent the last few months of his life shut up in an apartment with drugs and alcohol.

On June 9, 1982, Ronald Roberts was found shot to death in his automobile. Police reports later confirmed Ronnie, age thirty-nine, the victim of a self-inflicted wound to the heart. The suicide note left in his apartment alluded to the fact that he was anticipating a reunion with Rebecca, his older sister, who was killed in an airplane crash a few years earlier.

Could it possibly have anything to do with his relationship to Oral? It was no secret that the two did not have a close relationship during his adolescence. Oral's travels took him away from his son on numerous occasions. Ronnie tried not to allow his feelings of pity and longing for his dad to get the best of him. After all, his dad's work was important and that was just always understood. In the years prior to his death, Ronnie and Oral had developed a closeness, but the young son would not bend to his dad's way of thinking—instead, he broke.

Pat Boone, the entertainment celebrity figure, eloped at age nineteen and fathered four wonderful daughters. They were, in many respects, the model family. In spite of a strict set of rules, daughter Cherry became an anorexic, weighing only eighty pounds in her early twenties.

Karen Carpenter's story is just another example of the tragedy that can afflict our youth in today's turbulent society. From 1969 to 1981, Karen and Richard Carpenter gave America such hits as: "Close to You," "We've Only Just Begun," "Merry Christmas, Darling," "Rainy Days and Mondays," "Mr. Postman," and "Hurting Each Other." But could America even begin to understand the "hurting" Karen Carpenter was experiencing in her own life?

At thirty-one years old and a mere eighty pounds, her body was nothing short of a sack of skin over bones. In October 1981, after battling anorexia for five years, Karen summoned her best girlfriend to make an anonymous call to a New York therapist as a plea for help. Karen had kept bottled up inside her years of fears and hurts that would come to the surface after only six weeks of therapy. It was then that Agnes and Harold, Karen's mother and father, were called in to be a part of some interrogation with their daughter. Agnes truly believed that Karen, like millions of other young people, was dieting stubbornly and stupidly and that she really had no basis for her problem. Underneath it all, what was this frail young lady crying out for? "Karen needs a hug and needs to be told she is loved" was her therapist's response to Agnes. Could it possibly be that with assets between 5 and 10 million, what Karen wanted most was something money couldn't buy?

The Carpenters were not a family prone to affection in the way of hugging, kissing, and touching. This family did not go into depth about feelings, but Karen needed depth. It was on this very day in which that depth became reality in Karen's life. A willing Agnes moved toward the couch Karen was seated on and embraced her daughter with the biggest hug. That hug was the lifeline thrown to Karen but, in retrospect, maybe thrown a little too late.

On February 4, 1983, Agnes heard a thump upstairs. After she called Karen's name repeatedly with no answer, Agnes rushed to find her daughter on the floor with eyes still opened but no breathing. Richard was immediately called to the house. Rushing through the Downey, California streets that overcast morning, his worst fears came true. Only twenty minutes later, the doctors pronounced her dead at a nearby hospital (Adapted from *The Carpenters, The Untold Story,* by Ray Coleman).

Little Jeffrey seemed to be a bright student and a handsome blond-haired boy. But a family move near Akron, Ohio, coupled with his dad and mom's incessant fighting, caused Jeff, in his dad's words, to become "suddenly silent and sullen."

In high school, Jeff drank heavily and, by his own admission, had obsessive thoughts of violence and sex. Unable to share these torrid dreams with his dad, he later expressed them in a horrible way. Jeffrey Dahmer is America's contemporary cannibal, serial killer of seventeen young men. What went wrong? That question still haunts Lionel Dahmer, his father.

Mahatma Gandhi reached India's millions with his message of peace through nonviolence. Yet he had little influence over his son, Harilal. The great leader of Hinduism was shocked when his son converted to the Muslim faith! In fact, Gandhi described it in the press as a "false conversion."

When his mother lay dying, Harilal showed up drunk. The famous religious leader is remembered as saying, "Men may be good, not necessarily their children."

It is parents' worst nightmare when their kids turn out bad. Nothing gets the attention of any conscientious parent quicker than the thought of losing a son or daughter. How can we save our kids from ruin? What are the exact steps we can take to prevent a colossal tragedy in our own home?

In this book, we are going to make these "winning strategies" very clear. This is a parenting handbook you will repeatedly use and reference as you watch your children grow and as you attempt to navigate them to the right decisions in life.

As we all know, there are no Parenting 101 courses in college or at the university. Too often parents don't learn the preventative steps to save their kids from disaster until it is too late. Don't make that mistake. Submerge your mind and heart in the principles enunciated in this book.

In addition to having spoken to over 4 million young people in person and having counseled thousands, I myself, with my wife, Christie, am a parent of three (two of whom are teenagers). I know these principles work. They have worked in my home. In a sense, I feel as though I have been on a fifteen-year study assignment taking notes of what has and has not worked in saving our kids from disaster in the 1,032 cities where I have spoken throughout North America.

The other parents who have had the courage and strength to retell their stories in this book prove the vital steps of *How to Save Your Kids from Ruin.*

. . .

When an ostrich buries its head
in the sand to avoid unpleasant facts,
it not only represents an undignified
spectacle; it also constitutes
an irresistible target.

. . .

The beginning step of disaster prevention is for parents to get their heads out of the sand. Don't let the parental pride/denial bubble blur your vision of the needs of your own kids. It's time to answer the wake-up call.

Chapter 2

Wake Up, Mom and Dad
Step #1 — Don't Be Naive!

Immediately after I finished speaking to the 1,500 students at Bradley High School, Jody raced up to me with tears in her eyes, openly crying, as swarms of students milled about me. "My parents would not believe what was going on in my life, and I almost died," she said. Now a graduated senior and a survivor, her message was simple. It almost took her death to wake her parents up to what was really going on in her life.

Most parents I meet have a difficult time facing reality concerning their son or daughter. That is why I created "10 RUIN INDICATOR QUESTIONS EVERY PARENT MUST ASK THEMSELVES ABOUT THEIR KID(S)," which is discussed in chapter 3. In addition, there are two sets of ten questions each family should use to establish a point of communication among themselves. Again, look closely at these sets of questions in chapter 3. It is painful for any parent to think something may be going wrong with their child. There are many reasons why. I will discuss five of the more important ones.

1. We Blame Ourselves for Our Kids' Mistakes

There are cases where parents are directly responsible for a child going bad. We have seen that reflected in the television evening news which often reports cases in which some kids reflect very poor parenting. Furthermore, there are many areas where we as parents need to improve. Sometimes our behavior, or lack of it, is a primary reason why things are malfunctioning with our son or daughter.

However, there are scores of instances in which good parents wake up to a nightmare problem with their children, and they are *not* to blame. Get yourself off the guilt trip if you have not contributed to the difficulties your child may be experiencing.

Remember, every child still maintains their volitional will to choose as they so desire. Some kids make extremely poor choices and suffer those consequences.

2. We Feel Inadequate to Confront the Problem

I meet many parents in this category. They know or have a good idea something is not right with their son or daughter. They may even suspect the problem, *but* they are terrified at the thought of how to deal with the situation.

. . .

Before I got married, I had six theories
about bringing up children; now I
have six children and no theories.
—Lord Rochester, 1676

. . .

I remind parents that there is usually a solution to every problem. In addition, there are many qualified individuals who can assist a parent and family when they seem to be struggling the most. You are not alone. There are people who care and who can help. Pull the barrier down. Allow for caring input from people on the outside of your family unit.

3. We Want to Avoid the Social Stigma

This is a big problem with many middle- and upper-class homes. What will the Smiths say? Their son or daughter is not troubled as ours is. This fake, everything-is-OK front many families put on is possibly the very reason their own kids end up in a collision in life.

In one of my speaking engagements, the coordinator pulled me aside and explained how the senior pastor had become consumed with maintaining an artificial front. His daughter, Peggy, had become sexually active and had become pregnant.

His response was to hide the problem from his congregation. He feared that it might jeopardize his job. How sad! I would have done the exact opposite. I would have solicited the congregation's prayers, support, and love.

Too many parents are living a lie regarding the problems in their homes. Get honest, watch other people melt before you, and share the struggles they are facing.

4. We Feel We May Have to Compromise Our Position

This has been the answer for some parents. The art of parenting for them is wrapped up in "If you are going to smoke, do it at home." Or, "If you are going to have sex, here, take a condom with you."

Our kids test us every day to see whether our beliefs are really convictions with us. Many parents lack backbone and tumble when their children challenge their position. This leaves a child wondering what really is right and wrong. Instead of viewing their parents as being solid as a rock, they are like a melting flake of snow.

In spite of the relativism, situational ethics, and shifting cultural morals of our day, stand solid. Don't compromise. Certain things are right and certain things are wrong.

5. We Are Afraid We May Have to Become Open about Our Own Problems

I have proclaimed this from every lectern I have stood behind all over America: "Parent, get honest about your own problems with your kids." Extract from your life what you have done right and wrong. Kids love an honest parent who is not afraid to share his or her personal blunders. Open up.

Our kids genetically reflect those who birthed them. Their actions sometimes remind us of what we have done in the past.

Jody lives in an affluent suburb. Her parents did not want to face the fact that she was into drugs and crying out for help. Listen to this story in her own words.

From the time I was in kindergarten until I was in eighth grade, I had very few friends. I was picked on and called names. I had a very low self-esteem when I was eleven years old. I hated myself and my life.

My parents ignored all my problems and refused to accept the fact that I could get into drugs. When I was twelve years old and in the eighth grade, I met a group of kids who became my friends. For once, I felt as though people really liked me, and I had a lot of friends. One Saturday at the mall, one of the girls, Cinda, offered me a joint. I saw no reason not to accept it. I was open to any suggestions on how to change my life. After that one joint, I wanted more. I continued smoking marijuana for the next eight months. I also started dropping acid. I didn't see the harm in it.

One evening at a party someone mentioned to me the idea of doing heroin and acid. I thought I'd give it a try. That same night a person I thought was my friend died because of an overdose.

Throughout all of this, I had continuous fights with my parents and siblings. They refused to see I had a problem. I started asking my parents for help to stop doing drugs. They ignored me and said it was just a phase to get attention. I started thinking about death and had planned out in detail how I was going to commit suicide. I continued to ask my parents for help, but they ignored me. I would do cruel things to my siblings for attention. I would yell and scream at my parents so they'd pay attention to me. I tried on my own to get off drugs and couldn't do it. My parents didn't notice I was in trouble for almost a year.

I had continued to plan out my suicide and worked out a perfect suicide note to my parents. My best friend, Andrea, found my note and took it to a guidance counselor at school. She then hunted me down that day and found me in my bathroom running a hot bath as I was about to slit my wrists. She fought me to the floor and got the razor blade away from me. She informed my parents of what I was up to and had been doing. I was truly scared of what would happen. My parents then realized I needed help. We started family counseling.

When my freshman year of high school started, I was ready for a new life. I wanted out of the drug scene but couldn't do it myself. My second week of high school, I walked into the guidance office and told my counselor what I'd been into and wanted out. I needed help. I got involved in a school program that helped kids get off drugs. That same week my mom found two joints in my room and realized I was not just going through a phase. I was in true danger. Throughout my freshman year, I got help from friends and school but never professional help. I had stopped smoking marijuana but had a hard time giving up LSD. When my sophomore year started, I thought I'd be fine if I only did acid.

I didn't want to give it up. I was tripping on acid almost all the time. The beginning of second semester of my sophomore year started, and no one knew I was still on acid. About this time, my best friend, Andrea, was hit and killed by a drunk driver. I thought my world was coming to an end. A full year and a few months had passed since I started doing drugs. I had lied to my parents and friends constantly about it. I was tired of continuously hurting my family, so I decided to run away. Two days after I left, my parents found me and placed me in a psychiatric hospital. I didn't want to be there, but I knew I needed help. I was sure I'd never see myself graduate. After two months in a treatment program center, everyone was sure I was ready to go back home.

When I started school again, I had tremendous adjustment problems and more serious depression. One day in a family therapy session, my psychiatrist suggested I start taking Prozac. I had been off of drugs totally for almost three months at that time and was scared to take even prescription drugs. I gave it a try anyway. It helped. Even after all the bad things we've heard, Prozac helped me.

I've been clean for almost two years now. It'll be two years in March. I've stopped taking Prozac and am doing fine. Finally, my life is the way I want it to be. I have a solid future, free of drugs and deep depression. I lived through it and I see how much treatment has helped me. Even though my parents ignored the problem at the beginning, once they started helping me and believing in me, I was able to overcome my drug addiction. I graduate May 27, 1994. I made it. Thank God. Jody

Jody is alive and that's all that matters. Your child's health—mental, spiritual, and emotional well-being—are of paramount importance. Don't be naive. Now let's examine the next step.

. . .

Chapter 3

. . .

Where Are June, Ward, and the Beaver?
Step #2—Be Informed!

Remember the 1950s? Now look at our culture today. As the commercial jingle used to say, "You've come a long way, baby."

David Halberstam, the Pulitzer Prize award-winning journalist, presents a panoramic view of this pivotal decade in his 800-page book entitled *The Fifties*—a book I recommend you read.

It was a decade of Eisenhower, Dulles, Oppenheimer, MacArthur, Hoover, and Nixon. Harley Earl put fins on cars; Dick and Mac McDonald and Ray Kroc started a hamburger chain that would stretch around the world. Kemmons Wilson dotted the nation's roads with his Holiday Inns. Grace Metalious wrote *Peyton Place* and "Goody" Pincus led the team that invented "The Pill." This was the lovable era of "I Love Lucy." America was a wonderful, thriving place, experiencing many meteoric changes. The technological changes began an upheaval in American culture that hasn't stopped since. Bigger was better; cars each year continued to expand in size. Most Americans had a dream of a better life: owning their own home (their cost: between $9,000 and $18,000); their own automobile; living in a new invention called suburbia; and shopping in a large discount store called Korvettes, originally developed by Gene Ferkauf.

"Leave It to Beaver" lasted six years; "The Adventures of Ozzie and Harriet," fourteen years; and "Father Knows

Best," nine years. Describing the sitcoms, Halberstam writes, "There was no divorce. There was no serious sickness, particularly mental illness. Families liked each other, and they tolerated each other's idiosyncracies. Dads were good dads whose worst sin was that they did not know their way around the house and could not find common household objects or that they were prone to give lectures about how much tougher things had been when they were boys. The dads were, above all else, steady and steadfast. They symbolized a secure world. Moms and dads never raised their voices at each other in anger. There were no drugs. Keeping a family car out too late at night seemed to be the height of insubordination. No family difference was so irreconcilable that it could not be cleared up and straightened out within the allotted twenty-two minutes. Moms and dads never stopped loving each other" (David Halberstam, *The Fifties* [New York: Villard Books, 1993], 509–10).

Although pretentious, the '50s were much different than today. We find ourselves attempting to parent during major shifts in cultural and moral norms today.

In the 1950s, there was:

- *Next to no divorce.*
- *A high percentage of people attending church regularly.*
- *An entertainment media which presented much more wholesome values.*
- *School beginning each day with a simple prayer.*
- *No drugs and teenage alcoholism. (It was rare for a teen to commit suicide.)*

In the 1990s, the landscape has changed:

- *AIDS is now the sixth leading cause of death for youth fifteen to twenty-four years of age.*
- *Every ninety seconds a U.S. teen attempts suicide.*
- *One out of every four births is to an unmarried mother.*

- *The average age of first-time drug use among young people is thirteen years of age. Some kids start at nine, and one out of six kids between the ages of nine and twelve are approached to try illegal drugs, according to Partnership for a Drug-Free America.*
- *One third of the nation's children live apart from their biological fathers.*
- *Fifty-five percent of women work outside the home, according to the Labor Department.*
- *At least 2.5 million U.S. teens carry guns, knives, razors, or clubs to school, according to the Center for Disease Control. Up to 135,000 guns are carried into schools each day.*
- *The number of child abuse or neglect cases per year exceeds 2.7 million cases. According to the Child Abuse Prevention Center in Baltimore, Maryland, 1,383 children died from abuse or neglect in one year!*
- *There are more outlets for hardcore pornography in America than there are McDonald's restaurants, according to the National Coalition on Pornography.*
- *One aggravated assault every twenty-nine seconds.*
- *One robbery every forty-six seconds.*
- *One forcible rape every five minutes.*
- *One murder every twenty-one minutes.*
- *One motor vehicle theft every nineteen seconds.*
- *One larceny/theft every nineteen seconds.*
- *One burglary every ten seconds.*
- *One violent crime every seventeen seconds.*
- *One property crime every two seconds. (Source: Federal Bureau of Investigation's Crime Index).*

According to the Census Bureau:

- *More than 14 million single-parent families are in America. Their estimate is that six out of every ten children born in the 1990s will live in a single-parent home.*

- *Nearly 3.3 million American children—or about 1 in 20—currently live in a home headed by one of their grandparents. More than a fourth of those children, or about 867,000, lived with grandparents in a home where neither of their parents was present. The numbers are growing. Proportionately to their numbers in the population, between one half and three times more inner-city minority children live with a grandparent than do white children. Even so, about 60 percent of grandparents raising their grandchildren are white and, often, reasonably well-off financially or socially, California studies show.*

According to the Center for Disease Control:

- *Seventy-two percent of all high school seniors have had sexual intercourse.*
- *Nearly one-fifth—19 percent—have had at least four partners.*
- *Among high school students who are sexually active, only 45 percent report using a condom during their last sexual intercourse.*
- *The Center for Disease Control has received reports of 1,415 AIDS cases diagnosed in teenagers thirteen to nineteen years of age; 12,712 in young people twenty to twenty-four years of age—many of these were probably infected during adolescence. [Note: This is full-blown AIDS diagnosis. The CDC does not track HIV cases. Guestimates suggest 1.5 million Americans are infected—only God knows how many are sexually active teens].*
- *Three million teens have sexually transmitted diseases, including gonorrhea, chlamydia, herpes, and hepatitis.*
- *By the age of eighteen, the average American child will have seen 200,000 violent acts on television, including 40,000 murders, according to the National Coalition on Television Violence.*

This deteriorating cultural landscape means we must know how to communicate correctly and effectively with our kids. Ask yourself right now, "Can I effectively carry on a conversation with my children? Do I know how to talk with them in a way that we exchange ideas meaningfully?"

As parents, we have a tendency to talk *at* our kids, but not talk *with* them. Let's begin by assessing where your children are at in their personal lives. Where are you and your spouse in the realm of parenting with your children?

. . .

Someone has figured out that the
peak years of mental activity must be
between the ages of four and twenty.

At four, we have all the questions;
at twenty, we have all the answers.

. . .

It's time to ask some questions that will help you ascertain what the needs may be in your family. Get alone with your spouse and ask yourselves the following questions. Although it may be difficult, attempt to be honest with your answers. Write your answers down. By writing your answers down, you will develop the resolve to do something about the situation.

10 Ruin Indicator Questions Parents Must Ask Themselves about Their Kids

Set #1 — Questions for Parents to Ask Themselves

1. Does my child lie?

Yes / No

2. Is my child on drugs or alcohol?

Yes / No

3. Is my child sexually active?

Yes / No

4. Is my child associating with the wrong friends?

Yes / No

5. Does my child have the fortitude to say "no" to the things that will harm his or her life?

Yes / No

6. Is there anything I see in my child's life that indicates his or her sexual desires are not normal?

Yes / No

7. Does my child have any worries?

Yes / No

8. Have I helped my child become a leader or follower with his or her friends?

Yes / No

9. Have I helped my child identify his or her personal strengths/talents and weaknesses?

Yes / No

10. Have I taught my child to be tough with life's challenges and problems?

Yes / No

Perhaps you have discovered some scary answers. Don't be alarmed. *You must be honest with your answers.* If you are not honest with your answers, you cannot get to the remedy your children and your home need. I repeat, you must be honest with your answers.

By answering these questions properly, you will identify your point of need. The husband and wife should come together as a unit, not pointing the finger of blame at each other for what may be an apparent problem with one or more of their children. Become a team. Do not allow your child's problem to drive you apart or destroy your unity as marriage partners.

Begin by affirming to one another, "We will work together, without blaming one another, until our child's need is met." Repeat this vow to each other as you face the difficulties that may arise in helping your child.

Set #2 — Questions Kids Must Ask Themselves

1. Do I realize that I am not invincible?

Yes / No

Although I am only a kid and life seems fun, I am not invincible. I can be hurt by wrong decisions. I can be wounded. I can be arrested. I can be humiliated. I can be killed. And everything that can happen to me, I can through carelessness or wrong actions cause the same to happen to someone else.

2. Do I know the dangers and possibilities of diseases and death associated with STDs (Sexually Transmitted Diseases)?

Yes / No

AIDS is only one of twenty-one active sexually transmitted diseases now flourishing. Many have NO KNOWN CURE. Although I have read the statistics of these diseases, I am vulnerable if I am sexually active.

3. Do I realize that these diseases are most likely present in my circle of friends?

Yes / No

Although I may be of a different culture than other high-risk kids, I have to believe that one or more of my friends may have been promiscuous with someone who has been infected. A person can be infected and show no visible symptoms.

4. Do I realize I am subject to drug or alcohol addiction if I begin with only a few joints or a few drinks?

Yes / No

Although I know that a few joints or a few drinks on only a few occasions may not harm me, I realize that all addicts were casual users in the beginning. But when others could stop, they could not! That could be me.

5. Do I realize my character, which is the sum total of my characteristics, such as honesty, loyalty, truthfulness, purity, and trustworthiness, is extremely important and will be a determining factor of my life's course?

Yes / No

Although I hear and read of persons saying character is not important, I believe my character will be the moving force in my life. It will chart a course for me of happiness or despair, success or failure, and construction or destruction.

6. Do I understand that my position in life and my progress in life will be greatly determined by who I associate with, run with, hang-out with, and am friends with?

Yes / No

If I am friends with one who steals, I will steal. Although I must have friends in life, I must be very selective who my friends are. Either I will change them or they will change me.

7. Do I realize that I must work in whatever manner my parents and I agree on?

Yes / No

Work is a part of everyone's life, whether you are a child or an adult. Not to work is to effectively say that others must produce for me while I am lazy, self-serving, and unambitious. On the contrary, if *all* of our family members are workers, producers, and contributors, we will be successful, *together* or *separately.*

8. Do I understand that my life will have disappointments and delights, and I must be able to adjust to both?

Yes / No

Although I want everything in my life to be a delight, I realize that life is not always that way. I must be reconciled to the fact that everything that happens in my life will serve as a growing experience, if I handle it properly.

9. Do I know which abilities and gifts I have that can contribute toward my career development?

Yes / No

I realize there is no specific time that I must identify my life's career, but I will benefit more by deciding it as early as possible in life. I know I can always change it if I want to.

10. Do I understand that I have a "power source" for help in every area of my life, which is my personal relationship with God?

Yes / No

Even if my family *is* or *is not* close to God, I realize I must establish my relationship with God personally and by experience.

These questions will provide a wonderful opportunity of interaction between parents and their children. Carve out what we call in my home "Family Time," and use these questions as the bricks to build a strong foundation for your parent/child role together. Get honest with one another. Watch them work to produce positive results in your home.

. . .

Chapter 4

. . .

Do You Have An Ear?
Step #3—Start Listening!

One Sunday morning I was speaking in front of nearly 2,000 adults in an affluent church in the Southeast. I had just mentioned this important point in saving our kids from ruin: **START LISTENING!** I kept repeating the phrase for emphasis and meaning: "Start listening! Start listening! Start listening!"

I then followed my chorus: "Are you listening, Mom? Are you listening, Dad? Do you have time? Are you *really* listening?" I was getting my point across loud and clear.

Any good public speaker learns to read his audience, almost like you read the headlines of a newspaper. An audience will send you many cues, and in a nonverbal way, they will talk back to you while you are speaking. That morning, as in every time I speak, I was scrutinizing my audience very carefully, sending instant signals from my eyes to my mind that it was time to go on to the next point.

Since I have spoken so much, I have seen many surprising things happen during my speeches. People have passed out, laughed, listened intently, shouted at me, gasped, cried, taken notes, audiotaped, videotaped, and to my humiliation, a few have slept. One or two have almost died (perhaps it was my sermon).

Watching someone silently cry while you are speaking is one of the rare glimpses a person can see in this life. These are not the public give-me-attention criers. They are the

don't-notice-me-I'm-hurting criers. Their tears have, time and again, said, "I know. I've been through it. I feel the pain."

In the second row, the Hopkins family was crying, wiping their tears as they listened to me. I mean they were really sobbing. As I reiterated my point, Kevin Hopkins could not take anymore. He literally shot out of his seat, raced forward, and darted through the front auditorium door that had the bold EXIT sign above it.

The crowd froze. His slingshot exit meant far more to them than to me. They knew what the Hopkins family had been through. By the end of my address, I had almost forgotten the outburst. The pastor came to me and notified me the Hopkins family had inquired if they could talk to me.

As we sat together, they related the tragic events in the life of Carver, Kevin's older brother. Carver, like a lot of kids, had experienced problems with drugs. His father, Rick, told me their relationship was strained. When they attempted to talk, things ended in a major collision, with both of them screaming and threatening one another.

Slowly, Carver, with his brother watching, spun his own cocoon of silence. His room was at the end of the corridor on the main floor of the family home. Each family member nodded when I asked if they knew he had needed help. Again, their words expressed their mutual regret that they should have done something far more drastic much sooner.

On a Friday night, Kevin was watching TV in the family room, while Carver was in his back bedroom. Rick was away from the house, expected to return any moment. Carver's stepmother, Carolyn, was in a downstairs room.

Kevin indicated his brother had been sending out signals for days that he was very troubled and needed help. Please note, Carver was *not* saying, "I'm troubled. I need help. If you don't help me, I may not make it much further." In essence, he was demonstrating a plea for help by his daily groping around the house, his drug abuse, and his volcanic eruptions with his dad.

Finally, the moment came. Kevin spoke slowly, "While I

was watching TV, I heard Carver explode, 'I'll show you all!' I knew instantly that this was it. I jumped out of my recliner and ran down the hallway toward his room. As I turned the corridor, we collided head-on, and the gun went off. Carver fell right on top of me. The gunshot wound to his head caused his blood to spill all over him and me. Jerry, I watched his eyes roll back in his head. I knew he was dead."

Many times Kevin's cryptic sentence has reiterated itself in my mind, "Jerry, I watched his eyes roll back in his head. I knew he was dead." How can this family ever be totally normal again? The fact is, they can't. So I began to help them pick up the shattered pieces of their traumatic experience and attempted to put it all back together again.

Kevin bluntly exclaimed, "We weren't listening." Quickly, I looked at Rick and Carolyn to gauge their response to this admission. They shook their heads. Their tears seemed to confirm the reality that they didn't stop their world long enough to attempt to save their son.

START LISTENING. Are you listening, Mom? Are you listening, Dad? Can you hear your kids? What are they saying? Do you have time? If you don't listen to them, someone else will.

Focus with me on what is meant by the word *listen.* Most parents really do not know how to do that. They are so busy formulating their response or sermonizing to their kids that they don't know how to *listen* to them.

. . .

A speech is like a wheel —
the longer the spoke,
the greater the tire.

. . .

Listen to your son or daughter. You must understand the concept: "**listen** (lis'n) v.i. to use one's ears consciously in order to hear, *he listened at the door but couldn't tell what they were saying* / to pay attention to speech, music, etc., *listen to me instead of gazing out the window* / to be influenced by, *you mustn't listen to his threats or promises"* (*The New Lexicon Webster's Dictionary of the English Language* [New York: Lexicon Publications, 1991], 578).

Are you listening? What is on your child's mind? What concerns them most? What are their dreams? What are their worries?

Four Ways to Become a "Listening" Parent

Listening Step #1 — Simply "Shut-up" and Let Your Child Talk

This sounds very crude. I'm sorry, but it is true. You can't listen if you are talking. Zip it! Close your mouth and force yourself to let your child talk. Listen to their words. Examine the expression on their face as they convey their thoughts. By *listening* regularly and repeatedly, you will begin to get to *know* your child.

• • •

Talk and you say what you already know,
but listen *and you can learn something new.*

• • •

Your kids will talk with you if they feel you are a good listener. Recently, I met with a renowned person. As I waited in his executive secretary's office, I was a little nervous. I knew the power he possessed. When I was ushered into his presence, I became more nervous. Why? This learned, successful man barely said a word. He kept telling me to talk. He told me he wanted to know as much about me and what I did as he possibly could.

As I was going down the elevator that day after my appointment had concluded, I reflected on our meeting. I was embarrassed! It was so clear to me that I had done the majority of the talking. I learned something that day which I try quite hard to remember every time I meet with someone, particularly when I meet with my three children: *Let the other person do the talking!*

The smartest people I have met in the field of business or parenting are the quiet listeners. Conversely, the dumbest individuals have been the blabbermouths. Zip it and listen!

Listening Step #2—Structure the Time and Place to Listen

It is hard to talk next to a passing freight train! There is a time and place most appropriate to listen to your child. Find out where that place is. It may be fishing, at a private lunch or dinner, skiing, grocery shopping, walking in the mall, on the back porch, at a football game, on the basketball or volleyball court, or in a quiet bedroom.

One thing I do know . . . there is a time and place with your child and mine. Determine what locations and times are most conducive for your child's talking with you, and maximize on those.

Obviously, it would be ideal if there were a regular pattern to your *listening* time with your child. Generally, it is better if just one parent is present. There are times when both mom and dad can *listen* together. However, kids have a tendency to open up more with just one parent at a time.

Find the best time and place, and regularly establish an opportunity of *listening* with your child. You will fall in love with those moments.

Listening Step #3—Squelch All the Interruptions

Think for a moment . . . what or who is interrupting the *listening* time with your son or daughter? Identify those interrupters and make a commitment to stop them.

My son, Jeremy, now a teenager, came home the other day

and with great dismay told me how one of his friends at school was not going to the Kansas City Chiefs football game with his dad. He hurried on to tell me why. "His dad is going to take one of his business associates instead." He could barely believe it! "You would never do that to me, Dad!"

Yes, there are times when we need enjoyment with our friends, without our kids, but we have always made it a practice in our home to partner or "hang-out" with our kids first and our friends second.

I'd rather play golf, watch a football game, or go shopping with Danielle, Jeremy, or Jenilee than any one of my friends. I know my time with them is limited. Some day they will be gone, and all I will have left is memories. My *true* friends will always be there for me, and I for them.

Shut the telephone off, turn the TV off, turn the radio off, tell your friends you will catch up with them tomorrow, and get alone and *start listening* to your kids.

Listening Step #4—Inhibit an Explosive Response

When we become good listeners with our kids, we learn some things about them that can provoke a quick-tempered response. It will be extremely difficult, but hold your response until the right time.

I am not saying that our parenting relationship with our kids is a *one-way, their-way only* arrangement. Parents must, as we discuss in other sections of this book, discipline, correct, disagree, and confront. Sequentially, this should be after we have *listened* and gotten all the facts and sentiments our child is attempting to express.

· · ·

People who fly into a rage
always make a bad landing.
—Will Rogers

· · ·

Hold your anger. Hold your condemnation. Tune in on being an excellent listener.

The malady of our day is the alarming number of teens who commit suicide each year. I have seen this tragedy inflict pain on literally every kind of home. It leaves a parent dizzy with grief and despair. Suicidologists make it clear that the majority of young people who take their lives emit warning signs prior to their fatal death wish. *Listening* is a part of preventing this tragedy.

The following is a heartrending letter I received from Dawn, a mother, regarding her own daughter, Leslie.

As you have probably guessed, I'm yet another mother trying to pick up the pieces after my daughter Leslie's suicide on December 14. Indeed, Leslie had gone through a lot of your classic signs—a loner period, involvement in drugs. It all terminated when my house was raided for drugs, because her boyfriend at the time was returning to the house after Leslie and I left for school and work respectively, and selling pot out of her room. The case was dismissed as the narcotics agents really hadn't had enough evidence to "warrant" the warrant.

It was a turning point in our lives. I wanted to distance Leslie from her boyfriend and other peer influences, so I sent her to live with her sister in Portland. Leslie came off drugs and alcohol and threw herself into her studies. I kept as close as I could to her via phone and periodic visits. Last May, she returned home for Mother's Day. Our plan was for her to "put her toe back in the water" and see if she thought she could return home for good. It was not to be. She could see that she would cave in to peer pressure again. It was very hard for us, as we missed each other terribly, and to be honest, I wanted her home. It was a hard good-bye and the last time I ever saw her alive.

Kelly, her sister, said she was quiet for a while on the trip home, but then soon bounced back, back to her studies and projects at her school, including gardening and Sober Support groups.

Her grandmother, my mom, died in November, and she and Leslie were very close. Then Leslie got a letter that the aforemen-

tioned boyfriend was getting married. A slight tiff with her sister in the morning completed the scenario for the day. Her sister walked in at 2 that afternoon to find her on the floor, dying of a gunshot wound to her head. What really got to us was, after running down the events, we surmised she waited all day until she heard her sister's car pull in before she fired.

Like all parents, I'm shattered. I'll heal, but I'll never quit crying. Keep up your great work, Jerry.

You help parents like me sooth our own wounds by knowing you're out there trying to save kids like ours. Dawn

. . .

Ninety-five percent of all
the friction of daily life
is caused by mere tone of voice

When a man speaks, his words
convey his thoughts and his
tone conveys his mood

. . .

START LISTENING. START LISTENING. START LISTENING. START TODAY!

. . .

Chapter 5

. . .

I Don't Want to Go Swimming
Step #4 — Be Discerning!

Why is it that parents are generally the last people to find out when something is going wrong with their kids? Parents come to me with the amazing declaration that they have discovered some trauma their son or daughter has experienced.

BE DISCERNING! Sometimes kids lie about what is really going on. You can't always detect a lie from the truth apart from the unique gift of discernment. How parents need this gift!

Don't be gullible. If there is a problem your child is experiencing, face it. Don't hide from it. Whatever you do, don't pretend it is not there.

In a sense, you have to be a sincerely motivated detective with your kids. A parent should be well read and versed on the things facing kids today. When you are knowledgeable, they will know it. If you are ignorant to what's happening with them and their friends, they will be the first to know it.

Instead of my theorizing on your need for discernment, let me share a true story of a close friend of mine by the name of Daniel Doell, who is now dead. His story begs you to exercise discernment with your children.

Dan Doell

When little Rivercrest High School in Bogata, Texas, with 197 students discovered six students tested positive with the

AIDS virus, I knew our organization needed to respond to this burgeoning problem in the teenage community. Word Publishing asked me to produce a video entitled, "AIDS Among Teens." It was not an easy assignment, and one that would leave its mark on me for years to come.

It was decided that we would videotape HIV positive young people from across the nation and allow them to sound off. Mr. and Mrs. George Bergalis from their home in Florida retold the story of their daughter, Kim, who was infected with the AIDS virus by her dentist, Dr. David Acer. Hematologists from Los Alamos, New Mexico, matched the strain of her AIDS virus with Acer's blood. (A new study has suggested the CDC vastly overstated the DNA test results. Similar strains of the AIDS virus were found in the community. This raises the remote possiblity the patients were infected by someone other than Dr. Acer. We must remember, at this point, the CDC stands by its conclusion that the dentist infected his patients and the insurance company settled out of court for millions of dollars.) It was a pathetic story of a Florida University student who in time looked like someone from a concentration camp.

As we searched for the exact people to interview, we knew we needed an individual who had the AIDS virus, was young, and still had hope. A close friend of mine hosted a meeting in his home for me to meet Dan Doell.

Craig prepped me for my meeting with Dan. He told me that Dan's T-Cell count was 186 — a normal count is over 1,200. (The CDC typically classifies the diagnosis of fullblown AIDS as a T-Cell count lower than 200 with one or more opportunistic infections present). Although Dan's T-Cell count was terribly low, he had no opportunistic infections. In fact, Dan looked as healthy as anyone.

Quite honestly, I was very apprehensive about that first meeting. My contact with people with AIDS was about as familiar as viewing their pictures in one of the many magazines I received. I was removed from the woes of those infected . . . until I met Dan.

Was I ever impressed with Dan Doell! He was a brilliant, handsome, articulate thirty-year-old young man. I was surprised at how intelligent he was as he talked. I chided myself at being paranoid about our first meeting. I had cut my hand a few days earlier and the wound had healed. There was a scab covering my injury, yet I must have put four bandages on it before I left for Craig's house!

I even remember thinking on the way over if I should be so bold as to shake hands with Dan using my left hand. *No, I thought. That would be inappropriate. He would know I was treating him like a leper.* I prayed for God to give me wisdom and teach me exactly what He wanted me to know through Dan.

My wife, Christie, and I grew to love Dan Doell. I knew that night that we should feature his story on the video. Perhaps more important than locating the right person for our taping, that night began a close friendship between Dan and myself. When the night came for the taping, we planned for Dan to be placed in the center of the set with 100 teenagers literally draped around him. They had no idea Dan had the AIDS virus until during the taping, one of my questions prompted him to reveal his status.

Those kids' eyes got about as big as mine during my first encounter with Dan. Some of them froze; others seemed almost to be in a trance as he shared his story.

How did it happen? William Doell, Dan's father, was a successful physician in Grand Junction, Colorado, and had everything to prove it. The family enjoyed a beautiful house on a multi-acre spread. It was a spectacular homestead. There were horses, a fruit orchard, a large swimming pool, and loads of fun things for Daniel to do with his little brother, Dathan, and his cute younger sister, Desiree.

They were three picturesque kids. Miriam, their mother, made them her top priority. She was always there for them. The family attended the little, nearby Valley Church. It was their expression of personal faith, one that guided their actions on a day-by-day basis. The parents thought so much of the Valley Church and its aspiring potential that the Doells donated eight and one half acres. This would be prime land for future growth and development.

The young minister, Fred Fuller, had ambitious plans for that property. He was a progressive preacher. In fact, the deacon board had hired him, convinced he could take the church to bigger, brighter days. Fred was a lean man, who was always well groomed and concerned with his personal appearance. Balding in the middle, his black hair was thick on the sides with a slight tint of gray but always sprayed in that rather perfect ministerial style.

Fred, with his wife, Luanne, who was referred to as "Mrs. Fuller," preached each Sunday on the virtues of the Christian life. They seemed to represent solid values. His own son, Daniel, was graduating from high school as they started to enter the summer of 1978. The Fullers had three daughters, Abbie, their youngest, Judy, and Betty, an adopted but equally loved child.

They were proud of Daniel. During the graduation ceremonies, they beamed, and it was hard for them to fight back the tears. He was a handsome, young man, entering life with all its hardships and challenges.

Pastor Fuller was an observant man. He noticed, for example, Dr. Doell and Miriam were having marital trouble. Nevertheless, the Doells were still faithful to the church. In fact, the Doells' oversized swimming pool provided an excellent "alternative baptism tank" for the expanding, ill-equipped Valley Church. Fred would escort the new converts into the pool, transforming its luxury into something of a sacred spiritual experience.

Young Daniel Doell watched the minister and developed something of an affinity toward him. Fred responded immediately to Daniel, who had the same first name as his own son. He knew Daniel's dad was gone from the home frequently, and to the young teenager those absent days added up painfully. Finally, William decided that Miriam and he could not make their marriage survive. Accompanied by one of his female medical assistants, he sought out a new practice in New Mexico. He would leave for weeks at a time. Meanwhile, Miriam knew there was another woman taking her place. The stress was awful. In spite of it all, she roused herself into something of a surrogate father and mother for fifteen-year-old Daniel.

Daniel was an intelligent young man. Later, he would graduate from high school and college; and following his dad's footsteps, he would graduate from medical school and become a medical doctor. At fifteen, it was always great fun when the church crowd came over for a baptismal or after service meal and fellowship. The entire Fuller family would come over to swim.

Fred Fuller, as Miriam would later recall, was a bit unusual. He was the one who decorated the Christmas tree and supervised the decorations of his home. They would show that festive tree off to every parishioner who visited their parsonage. Fred was meticulous with the other interior decorations of his home. Maybe that was nothing, but in one sermon he talked about what a comfort it was when all the children finally arrived back at home late on a Friday or Saturday night. Everyone could relax. All was well. They could fall asleep in their "jammies."

Miriam saw these as small oddities of the minister. Nevertheless, she dismissed these thoughts and would not recall them again until later.

Fred Fuller would take church kids on retreats. These were overnight "spiritual camping escapades." Fred would tell parents that this was a time of ministering to the young lads, praying with them, instructing them in the ways of God. No one thought anything of it.

When Luanne Fuller had to make a trip to their hometown and William was on another one of his business trips, it seemed only natural that Pastor Fuller would invite Daniel to a "men's-only slumber party" at the parsonage. Fred told Miriam that his Daniel would be there, and perhaps he could be of comfort and encouragement to the young man.

How kind of the minister to think of Dan, Miriam thought. "Sure, he'd love to come."

Dan would later tell me that this one night seemed to forever disorient him and curse him with peculiar desires for years to come.

Pastor Fuller welcomed Dan at his home and said good-bye to Miriam. Where was his son Daniel? He too was away, leaving Daniel and Pastor Fuller alone at the house. As the evening wore on, they ultimately wound up in the pastor's bed — the same bed he shared with his wife Luanne.

Miriam related to me the way Pastor Fuller trapped Dan Doell now at age sixteen that tragic night (paraphrased):

"Touching is wonderful. God does not condemn. I love you, Daniel. This is what good friends do to comfort one another."

"Is this wrong?" Dan uneasily quizzed his pastor.

"No, Daniel, everything is fine . . . this is OK," Fred returned. "I've done this with other children too, Daniel."

In the privacy of that home, undisturbed by any outside interruptions, Dan Doell experienced his private hell. He would later tell me that Fred raped him.

When Dan was dropped off at his house that next day, the poor teen was deeply troubled. How did he sleep those next seven to ten nights when he told no one how this monster incognito had sexually molested him? The next Sunday Pastor Fuller was back in the pulpit exhorting people to live a good Christian life. How did Dan endure that last final sermon? What harrowing thoughts were tormenting him there in that church pew?

His dad was gone. He couldn't talk to him. Was this, after all, as Pastor Fuller had said, "OK"? Who would believe him? What was he? What was Pastor Fuller? Why did he do "that" to him?

This self-confident minister was ready to bring his family over to the Doell's pool for another swim just days after the molestation. Maybe he thought he could advance further with young Daniel Doell. After all, everything must seem to be "normal."

All was seemingly "normal" until Dan responded violently to Pastor Fuller coming to the house with his family for a swim. "I'm not going swimming!" Dan shouted out. "Why Dan?" his mother inquired. "I don't want to tell you!"

Miriam gently and lovingly persuaded Dan to reveal his apprehension for the activity in the pool that was soon planned to happen. It all came out. Dan retraced the night of the slumber party at the pastor's house.

Miriam was sick! Immediately, she called the elders of the church. There were only three in the small congregation. Within an hour, they rendezvoused at the Doell home. The lurid story came out.

Daniel Doell met with each of the elders individually and recounted the story identically each time. There was no doubt. The church had hired a pedophile!

That night the elders met with Fred Fuller, confronted him, and terminated him as their pastor. Fred Fuller, like many other molesters, denied every charge against him. However, he left town with all of his family and possessions within days. Where did he go? Probably, he went to another pastorate, and to another young boy like Daniel Doell.

When Dr. Doell found out about his son's molestation, he was furious! Good thing Fred was not in Grand Junction, Colorado at the time. William Doell was devastated.

Miriam and the three children traveled to the Kansas City suburb of Olathe less than one year after this time to find a new home and moved there a couple of years later. After twenty-three years of marriage, William and Miriam Doell divorced, leaving Dan and his siblings in a single-parent home.

Dan made it clear to Miriam, me, and others that the molestation he suffered from the hands of his pastor made him think he was homosexual. To have attention, sex, love, and acceptance from someone of the same sex blows your mind.

Dan enrolled in a Christian college and secretly started cruising gay bars. Later, Dan met Andy, a jewelry salesman who was ten years his senior. They became roommates and lovers. In 1983, after prolonged illnesses, Dan checked Andy into a Kansas City hospital. He had to have a hernia operation. Andy never made it back to the apartment. He returned to his parents' home in another state for the holidays. He survived only through Thanksgiving. After his death, the doctors informed Dan that his friend had died from complications brought on by G.R.I.D.S. (Gay-Related Immuno Deficiency Syndrome) as it was termed then. This was just two years after the CDC started investigating a new virus that was racking up a death toll like a small war.

Andy had been with many partners, but never told Dan that he was infected. After Dan was tested, he too proved positive with the AIDS virus. He was shocked.

Later, after moving back home with his mother, Dan received another blow. Having completed years of education he received a medical doctorate. The hospital he was to work at learned of his diagnosis when Dan himself divulged all the facts. As a result, the hospital voided his contract and asked him to sign a waiver saying that he would agree to resign. As a renewed, dedicated Christian, Dan felt morally obligated to comply.

Dan spent the final years of his life treating AIDS patients in a clinic. One day I observed him treating those dear people in different stages of sickness and disease. He was extremely kind, and he was their favorite. He truly was one of them.

On February 10, 1994 at 2:06 A.M., Dan took one final breath. He had been relatively free from many of the opportunistic infections people with the AIDS virus suffer from. But in those last days, he did suffer. His final weight was only eighty-five pounds, and it had become a battle just to breathe. Oxygen, a compassionate measure, helped relieve the strain of breathing greatly. But nothing could save his life.

Two weeks earlier, on Saturday, January 22, 1994, while Dan was still being attended to at home by his mother, he experienced three "grand mal" seizures at 7:20 A.M., 2:10 P.M., and 4:10 P.M. Miriam said, "Blood poured from Dan's mouth and nose, soaking seven large Pamper diapers. His mouth was full of blood." Had they not rolled Dan to his side, he could have drowned.

After Dan was rushed to the hospital, a CAT scan revealed he had "toxoplasmosis," a disease associated with cats. Miriam feels confident in that horrendous day of January 22, Dan experienced at least two strokes. The right side of his face and body seemed impaired for the few days he had left.

Just days prior to Dan's death, I went to the facility where he was. It was a grim sight. Standing over his body, memories of the times we spent together raced through my mind. One joyous night, Dan, along with four of Christie and my closest friends, took a charter flight to Tulsa where I spoke that evening. I noticed Dan was wearing my long camel hair coat I had previously given him. As we flew home on the plane, he sat opposite of me. I kept looking at him in that plane seat, drinking a cola, laughing, and having a good time. I knew those good times for him would not last forever. And they didn't.

Dan tried to communicate with me in that hospital bed. But because of the AIDS virus, the mental dementia caused even speaking to be almost an impossibility for him. How he tried though! I will never forget us saying to him, "It's OK, Dan, we love you. Let go, friend. Go ahead and let go. You are going to a better place. We love you."

Standing there, viewing his ravaged body, I thought of Pastor Fred Fuller. Where was Fred Fuller now? How many more children had he destroyed? Fred Fuller didn't care. His Daniel, no doubt, was alive and well. His Daniel was married, no doubt had children, a nice job, and was enjoying the American dream.

When Dan was in the height of his gay lifestyle, one night he called Fred Fuller and told him what he was and what he was doing. How did Pastor Fuller respond on the other end of the phone that night? I don't know. No one does. Does he ever wake up in the night and think of young Daniel at age fifteen in that house of his? Does he care? I sincerely doubt it.

The radiologist informed Dan's mother that there were four things which could have caused his actual death:

(1) The "toxoplasmosis" infection.
(2) The "cyto-megalo" virus, an infection in his eye, which had damaged his sight and was threatening his brain matter.
(3) Cancer.
(4) The AIDS virus itself, which had conquered his immunity system.

The image that showed up on the CAT scan of Dan's brain was a mass 1" to 1½" in size and could have been caused by any one of the four listed possibilities. The radiologist indicated this mass had displaced and shifted brain tissue in the frontal lobe.

Dan's body was cremated. At his memorial service, approximately 200 friends and family members were present. It was a bitterly cold, early March night. I spoke and shared my thoughts about Daniel Doell. His dad, William, was unable to attend, but the following is a part of the letter William wrote to be read that night:

> Some of you at this memorial service knew my son better than I. In his formative years, I was a workaholic, as had been my father before me. That is not an excuse, however, that is just a fact of life. When he was fifteen, I was gone. Our contact for the next six to seven years was only cursory at the very most, with greeting card notes on the appointed days. Dan accomplished much on his own. He put himself through college, two years of dental school at the University of Missouri and then four years of medical school. I emphasize that he did that on his own. He was proud of his

accomplishments. . . . When we did get back together for the first time in 1986 at a medical meeting in Texas, there was an obvious veil between us. I suspect that he knew he was carrying the dreaded AIDS virus. He bore that knowledge alone for maybe one to two years, which had to be a very lonely time for him. In the intervening years, some of the layers of that veil slipped away, but thin as it had become, the veil was still in place. My hope is that Dan discovered who I was as a physician during the preceptorship that he spent in my office in Denver.

Then I hope that Dan discovered who I was as a more mature father during the four months this past year when we tried to help him regain his health. In the end that was not to be. . . . I'll see you on the other side, son. I love you.

Dad.

Parents, be discerning with your children. It is *not* "danger-stranger" in 90 percent of the cases who takes advantage of children. It is someone you know; someone they know. It can be a family member, a neighbor down the street, a teacher, a Sunday School teacher, even a pastor.

My motive is not to cause hysteria among you. Travels have taught me to be very discerning with people. I want to protect my children; you need to also.

BE DISCERNING!

. . .

Chapter 6

. . .

I'm Dying to Talk with You
Step #5—Start Talking!

Have you ever sat in a restaurant or an airport as I have, and watched two best friends talk? What a sight to see! I don't know if even a stenographer could keep up with many of them. Great friends love to talk. They talk about everything and everyone.

Do you talk with your kids? Would they pick you as that one person they would most like to talk with? If not, why not? If we are going to save our kids from ruin, we must start talking with them. We must create a communication "Super Highway" between them and us on every matter important in their life.

If your kids can *talk* with you, they will *tell* you when they are having problems. You will be able to intervene. You *can't* talk if you are gone all the time. Remember, talking requires time. **START TALKING!** Tell them you want to become their best friend.

When my son, Jeremy, now a teenager, was five I asked him very seriously to become my best friend. He said he would. All these years he has truly believed we *are* best friends. One time, after disciplining him for almost killing his little sister, Jenilee, he looked at me amid tears and asked, "Dad, are we still best friends?"

"Jeremy, we will always be best friends."

What does Jeremy love the most? When just he and I get alone together and talk! **START TALKING.**

. . .

*It is more important to get
the first thought
than the last word.*

. . .

A Dad Who Heard His Daughter Call

Dr. Paul "Tex" Yearout has spoken to over 7 million young people in 6,000 public junior and senior high schools and colleges in every U.S. state, every Canadian province, and Europe. He is one of the finest communicators to young people I have ever met. Tex's organization, Youth Enterprises Agency, based in Yakima, Washington, has held Family Life Seminars and provided help to hundreds of thousands of parents internationally.

In the beginning it was my dear friend Tex who taught me how to speak on the public school campus. He helped me understand the setting and gave me invaluable communication skills. I would not be where I am today without his assistance.

When Tex visited Kansas City on his numerous speaking tours, he stayed in our home. My brother and I looked to Tex as a best friend. It started when we were in high school. During the summer, he would come speak at our camp. He was our favorite speaker. All the kids loved Tex. He was a hit! He was so real, so penetrating, and so funny. Jeff and I would connive our way into his speaker's quarters. We wanted to talk with Tex. No one was better at *talking* and listening to kids. We kept him up late, and the weary warhorse did not mind.

On one of my trips to Portland, Oregon years later, Tex told me a gut-wrenching story of his own daughter's struggle to survive. Watching tree logs float down the Clackumus River and listening to Tex share his sad story, I could barely believe my ears. Tex was "Mr. Parent." If it could happen to his daughter, his family, I guarantee you, it can happen to yours and mine.

Tex and Peggy Yearout have three children: two boys and one darling daughter by the name of Sandy. Although Tex and Sandy were inseparable, Tex almost lost Sandy to ruin. This is his story.

When I learned I was a father of a little girl that was the crowning joy, because I had two wonderful sons, and I never believed that God would be so wonderful as to give me a little girl. I was so excited.

We know the importance of a father-son relationship, but I learned also that it's vital to have a father-daughter relationship because young girls between about thirteen and fifteen years of age absolutely require the love of a man in their life. Now that man ought to be their father in a proper, beautiful, wonderful father-daughter relationship. If the girl does not have this, she doesn't really know what's missing in her life and what she's hurting for, so she reaches out to guys—usually guys much older than she is and those guys exploit her.

I knew all this. I also knew that I couldn't have any kind of relationship with my daughter when she was a teenager if I didn't have one before. You don't wait until they're teenagers when suddenly they've got problems, hassles, and rebellion, and then say, "Hey, now we're going to start talking." If you haven't talked before, you're going to have a difficult time ever talking then. God gives us twelve years to get ready for adolescence and a lot of us blow it.

So I started from infancy entering into the care of this little girl when I was at home, changing diapers (I did it with my boys too), giving her a bottle, loving her, taking her around, and being proud of her. Then as she got to be a toddler, I'd come home from one of my trips, and my wife would say, "I'm going to go out and have lunch with some of my friends, and you can take care of Sandy." I was delighted.

Sandy and I built a beautiful relationship as father and daugh-

ter. We could talk. I took her shopping . . . and all kinds of things which I did with my sons too. I also would take her on speaking engagements with me. We had a great relationship—just wonderful communication. All of my kids felt free to tell their mother and me whatever was going on in their lives . . . about their friends, about things that were going on. They never felt they had to be secretive or hide because we didn't ever penalize them for telling the truth.

At the end of June 1983, after Sandy's high school graduation, I went to Vancouver for some youth ministry. I took Sandy along, and we had a wonderful time. As we shared about the Lord, she shared about her plans. She wanted to prepare herself to work with troubled kids and go on to college. I was excited as we had a great time together. After we came home, I walked around, patting myself on the back, saying, "Well, Yearout, praise God. Your last one is now on her way, and she loves the Lord. Thank You, Lord." Two months later, disaster happened.

There was a young girlfriend of my daughter's who also went to the Christian school. Her friend had begun going with a non-Christian guy, who lived a pretty rough life. Sandy had constantly talked to me about this situation, and I knew the girl very well. Sandy and I would often pray for her friend, that she'd open her eyes so she wouldn't mess up her life.

Early in August, this young man left for the Marine Corps, and his parents were having a going-away party for him. Sandy was not a party attender, but her friend asked her if she would come to this going-away party. Sandy went with the whole idea of winning this kid to Christ before he left for the Marine Corps. She took her Bible and went to that party.

At the party that night was a young man by the name of Keith, an aspiring young rock singer who had been brought in to entertain. He wrote most of his own stuff, and Sandy said that when he would finish some numbers, all the girls would run around him. She ignored him, and I guess it got to him and finally he sought her out. One of Sandy's gifts is writing, and since he wrote all of his own stuff, they talked about their mutual interest in writing.

At the end of the party that night, he came to her and asked if he could come over to her house. She said yes. So the next afternoon he came to the front door. She got her Bible, went to the door, and met him. Then they went out and sat on the steps, and she shared Scripture with him. He seemed to be receptive. The next day he came back, and they took a walk, and again she took her Bible and shared more Scripture with him. She was working at Kentucky Fried Chicken at the time and getting ready to start junior college here in Yakima, but since she was spending more and more time with him, I asked her, "Sandy, could you tell me what's going on?"

"Oh, nothing, Dad. I'm just trying to win this guy for the Lord. In fact, could he come over to the house and sing a couple of the songs for you and Mom that he's written?" she asked.

I said, "Well, OK."

He came to the house a couple of nights later and brought a little amp in and his guitar. The minute he walked in and I met him, I died. Now I've worked with people my whole adult life, and I can read people pretty well. I want to tell you that he had the most evil eye and aura about him that I have ever sensed in any human being I've ever been around. The very presence of Satan was obviously in this man.

He sang a couple of his songs, and then he said to Sandy, "Let's go."

Well, out of force of habit I said, "When are you going to bring her home?"

Since he was twenty-one and she had just had her eighteenth birthday, he looked at me like he thought I was insane, and she looked at me like "Dad?"

"I still want to know when you're bringing her in," I said. He mumbled something about 1:30. I said make it 12:30. He brought her in at 2:30.

Then everything started going downhill. All this beautiful communication that we had was gone. He hung around the Kentucky Fried Chicken. He was there constantly keeping her under surveillance while she was at work. The minute that she would get home, he'd be at the door demanding her. We'd say, "Well, she's in taking a shower." He'd run around and try to break into her bedroom window. It got worse and worse. I'd try to talk with her, and she'd just go to her room.

Finally she took one of her friends to get her hair fixed. She had a little pickup I'd bought for her to drive to school. Sandy took her friend to a hair appointment and told the friend she'd come back and pick her up. When the friend got through she came out to pay the bill. Sandy had left her a note and the keys to the pickup. Sandy wrote, "I'm running away. Tell my parents I have to get away, and I'm going to be gone for a while. I have to get away from them and Keith, and get my head straight."

After Sandy's friend called us, we got the pickup, brought it home, and I thought, well, that's good. Maybe she can get away and God can deal with her. She's away from the pressure of us and the pressure of him, and maybe that's for the best. But I was heartbroken. None of my kids had ever done this before. It just tore me apart.

It was a Wednesday, and about 5:30 that afternoon, Keith showed up at the door and demanded, "Where's Sandy?"

I said, "I have no idea."

"What's that supposed to mean?" he asked. I thought maybe I could really talk to this guy.

I went outside, shut the door, and said, "Keith, why are you so interested in my daughter? Why are you so focused in on her and so determined to break her relationship with me and her mother and our family? What do you want to do? You want to turn her into some dirty, cheap little tramp like most of the girls who tragically you've been with, then after you've had your victory, dump her. Is that what you've got in mind? I don't think you've ever been around a Christian girl before, and you probably don't understand where she's coming from."

He said, "I don't have to stand here and listen to that."

I said, "No, that's true, you don't. As far as I know, she may be jumping into the Yakima River because kids do that sort of thing when they get under this kind of pressure."

"Well, I'm going to go find her," he said.

I was upset. He had a little Opal car that he drove. It's the worst piece of junk I have ever seen. He went to his car, and I followed him. I wanted to provoke a fight. The Bible says, "Revenge is Mine, says the Lord." I said, "God, use me as Your instrument. I poked him in the chest with my finger as hard as I could. I said, "I want to tell you something. If you violate my daughter or touch her or harm her in any way, you are a dead man." Well, that wasn't a Christian speaking; that was a father speaking.

He said, "Old man, you're not going to be able to even live in this town much longer."

I said, "Get off my property!" So he left.

That night I went to our church where one of our pastors is an ex-policeman and unofficial chaplain of the police department. I got him out of the service, went into his office, and I broke down and wept. I told him what all was happening. I asked, "Do you think you could find out if there's a record on this guy?" And he said, "Sure." He called the police department and talked to some of his friends down there, and they went to Records and looked Keith up.

After he hung up the phone, he said, "Well, Tex, he was on drugs and alcohol from the time he was twelve years old until he was eighteen. During this time, he committed four felonies. At age eighteen, he was facing prison or going to a mental institution. Since his father is a professional counselor in the Yakima area, he was able to send him to Medical Lake (a mental institution). He was there two years. He was home only a few months when Sandy met him. A month before she met him, the Yakima police had picked him up on a hidden weapons charge. But again, because of the father's influence, he was allowed back on the street."

We were pretty sure where Sandy had gone. We called the girl's home where we thought she had gone and I told her this stuff about Keith because I was scared. Sure enough, Keith found her. He figured out where she was too.

Two days later she came home, and the first thing she said to me was, "Dad, you and Dave Kelly are in big trouble."

I said, "Oh, how's that?"

She said, "Well, because I know how you found out all that stuff about Keith—through Dave Kelly and his connection with the police department. That's privileged information. So Keith and his dad are going to sue you."

I was ready to throw Sandy out of the house because she was coming in at 4 in the morning, while working at Kentucky Fried Chicken, and getting ready to start college. None of my kids had ever done that. The tendency is to say, "I've had it with you. If that's how you want to live, you're going to live somewhere else." Thus I was about ready to say to her, "If you like this guy so much, you're out of the house."

But then I met Keith's father and he told me, "If you ever kick her out of the house, she's welcome in our home." This checked me.

I had been booked to speak at Westside Family Camp which they have every Labor Day weekend. Before they had always booked guys from the seminary with Ph.D.s. They had asked me to be the speaker over that Labor Day weekend and I was quite honored. Nevertheless, I felt so guilty that I called the pastor and his wife. After they came over to our house, I told him what was going on. His wife really loved Sandy. "Tim," I said, "I'm not going to speak that weekend. I'm not fit. In fact, I'll never speak again. I'm quitting the ministry. I'm not worthy."

He was a wise pastor, and he said, "Tex, Satan is not only trying to destroy Sandy, he's trying to destroy the ministry you've had all these years with kids. You are going to speak at that weekend, and you're not going to quit preaching!"

I've never preached with a greater broken heart in all my life than that weekend. God did some neat things in some people's lives that weekend. This was the first part of September, and Sandy began to go to school. Meanwhile, this guy started hanging around the school, hanging around our house, and I hated to leave my wife with all of this. One night she invited him in. My wife has a great ability to keep her cool. I mean I get emotional, but she can really handle it. She brought Keith in and talked to him for an hour and a half. We were on the phone every night for an hour to an hour and a half, crying, praying together, and sharing the Scripture. I tell you, nothing will drive you to the Word like an experience like that. In early October I flew into Pasco, Washington. I told Peg to bring Sandy and Butch, one of my sons, and meet me down at the airport. We would go out for a nice dinner. I got in at 8:30 that evening. My wife and my son were there, but Sandy didn't come. I didn't even ask them why she didn't come, and they didn't say. We went to a restaurant and just kind of played with the food and went home. We got home about 10 P.M. and walked into the living room. Laying on the dining room table was a note from Sandy to me. It said,

> Dear Daddy: I love you. I love you. I love you. I love you! I need you more than I've ever needed you in my life. I need your strong arms around me, but I am so ashamed of myself that I couldn't face you tonight. So I went to a motel. After I get out of school tomorrow at noon, I'll come home, and we can talk. I will call you.

She did call, and I tried to get her to come home, but she'd already paid for the room. I didn't sleep that night because I remembered how every time we'd try to talk, it always ended up in me yelling and her walking off. So I prayed, "God, please help me know what to say."

*When she came home at noon, we greeted one another with a hug and a kiss. I took her down to the Holiday Inn where the waitress came and took our order. I'll never forget this as long as I live. I think I'll even remember it in eternity. She looked me right in the eye and said, "Dad, I've got a solution to the problem." I said, "What is it, honey?" She said, **"Will you run away with me?"** A million thoughts flashed through my mind. You know, like how in the world can I do that? I've got all these bookings out here. But God said to me, "How many fathers have you told across America, if your teenager needs you, you'd better be available, even if it costs you your job?" And I thought, hey, what's more important? So we lose the home; so we lose the car; what's the difference? She's worth everything.*

So I said, "Honey, you've got it, but we do have to tell your mother." She said, "OK, but nobody else."

This was Tuesday, and she said, "Dad, I'll keep going to school the rest of the week, working at Kentucky Fried Chicken. I'll go out with him every night like I've been doing. Then Saturday night when he brings me in and leaves, I'll have my stuff packed, and then we'll leave."

I said, "OK." She was so frightened.

She was in mortal terror as we left Yakima. She was afraid that he would find her. We got out of town, and she just went to sleep like a baby. About 6 in the morning we stopped at a motel and got up about 2 in the afternoon. We drove around Oregon, living off my credit card. They're wonderful, you know!

When we left early Sunday, Peg was extremely upset. We have a little recording device with our telephone so that we can put it on to receive calls if we're not there or don't want to be bothered. You can set it so you can hear the caller. He started calling that morning about 9. Every thirty minutes he would call, curse at the machine, and then yell. Finally, about noon, she took the phone and talked to him, saying, "Keith, at her request, Sandy and her dad left this morning."

"Where did they go?" he shouted.

"I don't know," she said, "and I don't want to know."

"When are they coming back?" he demanded.

"I don't know, and I don't want to know."

Keith harassed both my sons and my wife, sent repairmen to our house, and also a message that he'd been killed.

Finally, my wife and son went down to the police department to talk to one of the detectives. They knew the guy. They told him what was going on and said, "Can't you do something?"

He said, "No, not until he breaks the law. We have to catch him on your property, or if he hurts one of you, we will take action."

But he said, "I'll call him and try to scare him." The detective called Keith and tried to scare him and get him to leave them alone. Keith told the detective that Sandy was eighteen, that they were engaged to be married in a few weeks, and that I had kidnapped her.

Then the police began to harass my wife because they said, "If your husband kidnapped your daughter, that's a crime, and we have to investigate it."

Sandy and I were just floating around the first week. After about a week, while we were in a restaurant, I looked at Sandy and said, "Honey, we have to talk."

She said, "Dad, I can't."

I said, "Honey, we have to talk." It was like a dam breaking—for an hour she sat there, and it just poured out. I was astounded at what I heard. For one thing, they were sitting out by the Yakima River one night in her little pickup. There was a fog hanging over the river, and all at once a patch of fog left the river, came, and started to surround the pickup. They were just sitting there and not talking. After the fog surrounded the pickup, he said, "I made the fog do that."

She said, "Oh, come on. Do you think I'm stupid?"

Keith replied, "OK, I'll make the fog go back," and it did.

She said, "It was the wind, probably. It had nothing to do with you."

He said, "OK, I'll make it come back," and it did.

She said, "Dad, suddenly it fully impacted me who I was dealing with." I said to Keith, "There are only two sources for that kind of power: Satan and God. You don't have God's power so I believe you have Satan's power." Keith threatened Sandy that he would kill her family. She was terrified.

When Sandy and I came home, she talked to Keith and told him it was over and that she didn't want to see him anymore.

But that wasn't the end. He kept harassing us by peeking in the windows, staking out our house, and following her where he could find her. After she went back to school in January, she'd be in a classroom when she would look up and see him looking through the window. She'd go into the student lounge area, and he would be behind the greenery, staring at her. She wouldn't sleep in her room for weeks after we got home, she was so frightened. Finally, she went to the president of the college with a couple other kids. He ordered Keith to stay off the campus. Then Sandy said, "Dad, I want to get out of Yakima." So she went to George Fox College, where she started midterm in January. Nevertheless, she was still struggling.

We kept getting the word that we were going to be killed, and finally we said, "Hey, you know, God is in charge of our lives, and if that's how we get to heaven, so be it. You can't go around looking over your shoulder the rest of your life."

Sandy went on to George Fox College, and God really worked in her life. She came home in March and said, "I can never go back to church again because everybody will look at me as if I'm weird." Most people in church didn't even know what was going on, and those who did loved us and prayed for us. Had it not been for the support of our pastor, our pastoral staff, of people who came and prayed and cried with us, we couldn't have survived.

In March of 1985, Sandy gave her testimony in our church, and then we left in June and went to New Zealand and Australia on a missionary tour. It started out by me having her give a brief testimony and speaking. It ended up with her speaking, and me giving the invitation. I thought she'd been to seminary, the way she used the Scripture. Boy, did she open up. Although she was a half a world away from home where nobody knew her, did she ever minister to kids in New Zealand. It was incredible how God used her to touch their lives.

Sandy spoke about her experience by saying that she was a teenager in trouble. Two years ago, she had no hope. She had turned her back on her parents, on her church, on her Christian friends, and she was heading down the road of destruction. She said, with parents like hers, raised in a Christian school, how in the world could she have problems. But, she confessed, she really rebelled, and it could happen to anybody. When she was rebelling, involved in some really bizarre things, if it hadn't been for her parents not giving up on her, she'd be on the streets today. She had a message for parents there and everywhere. She said

> If you've got a kid going through some hard times, and they're turning against you and they don't come home at night, don't give up on them. You want to kick them out. You want to just let go of them and say, "OK, fine. Go your own way. I'm washing my hands of you." Please don't do it. Pray for them. Pray that the Lord brings someone into their life. He brought someone into my life, and it was because my mom and dad both prayed for me.

Thank the Lord. He provided a way for Sandy to go to George Fox College. I'd like to challenge you as a father, not that you are going through what we went through, to look at your own children, your wife, the home, and you as the leader. And maybe some of you dads need to sit down with your children. Maybe you need to apologize to them for some attitudes. Maybe you need to verbalize how much you really love them. You're the leader.

People ask me, "Where is Sandy today? How did she turn out?" Thank God, great! In fact, she married her high school sweetheart on July 12, 1986. They are extremely happy, very involved in an excellent church, and the proud parents of Katie Jean. She is a little gem. God has been so good to us—He took something bad, and turned it around to something very good.

I am so glad Tex Yearout heard his daughter's cry for help and *didn't give up on her.* He heard it because for years they had been talking. **START TALKING** with your child today.

. . .

Chapter 7

. . .

Three Squeezes Means...
Step #6 — Embrace Them!

One teen sent a letter to me and shared how her parents never expressed their love verbally to one another or to her. She indicated it really bothered her. She wanted to hear her mom and dad say, "Stacy, we really love you." It never happened.

Her response was that she went out of her home seeking someone who would express his love for her. She wanted to hear it and feel it. It wasn't long until she was in with a crowd at school that was into partying and drinking. She was in the middle of the revelers, getting loaded with her friends and having sex with one guy after another who reaffirmed his "love" to her.

After being "used and dumped" over a period of months, she came home one day to find her parents were away. Reflecting on the misery of her life, she roamed into her parents' master bedroom and then into their bathroom. Standing there in a delirium, thinking of how messed up her life was, she noticed something in the wastebasket. It was a Kleenex with which her mother had removed her lipstick the night before and tossed away.

She related in her letter that she carefully extracted the Kleenex out of the wastebasket and closely observed the fine features of her mother's lips, indelibly engraved on the tissue. Stacy came to the realization in that moment that almost all of her problems with drugs, alcohol, and sex came when she *thought* her dad and mom really didn't love her enough to tell her. They had never put their arms around her neck and shoulders and hugged her. She longed for their physical embrace.

With great care, she folded her mother's discarded Kleenex and revealed in her letter how she carried it to school with her every day. When she got to the loneliest points of the day, knowing there was nothing really to live for, she would take her mother's Kleenex out of her pocket. Stacy would gently unfold it and press her mother's lip mark against her cheek!

Embrace Them!

Your kids are waiting for you to embrace them. Do it today! Tell them several times a day how much you love them. Be sure to embrace them. Give them a hug. Hold their hand. Write an affectionate note and slip it in with their lunch. Place it on their pillow or on their mirror. You'll never know what a consolation and comfort your "love squeezes" will mean to them.

Some studies seem to suggest that the absence of physical love and affirmation can have devastating consequences on our children. We must affirm them. When our kids face problems, we need to become their cheerleader.

Tiffany, Don't You Remember?

Tiffany Delaney, seventeen, was a beautiful blonde teenager who, with her brothers and sisters, had appeared in several commercials—Gerber Baby Foods, Mattel, Coca-Cola, and Kool-Aid, among others. This vivacious cheerleader was nicknamed "Barbie," at her high school. She was gorgeous. Soon all of that would change.

On January 27, 1989, Tiffany was driving with her sister,

Sabrina, at approximately 6:30 P.M. on Topanga Canyon Boulevard in California, when Anders Leif Grunberg, came barreling down the road at 55 miles per hour. Grunberg crossed the double yellow line and smashed into Tiffany's white Volkswagon convertible. Twelve-year-old Sabrina was riding with her big sister. Tiffany had fractured legs, lacerations, and was airlifted to Northridge Hospital.

Grunberg was driving without a motor vehicle license, and he was intoxicated. After the accident and prior to becoming a fugitive, he called the police station, not to check on Tiffany's condition, just his car. The wreck was severe. Tiffany had been catapulted out of the car and came to rest by the left door of the vehicle. The left rear tire of the car was on Tiffany's hair holding her down on the ground.

While Grunberg escaped from the country and the law, Tiffany wound up comatose in a hospital bed for five long months. She was left unconscious and was not expected to live. Her mother and father, Pam and Larry Delaney, however, would not give up on their daughter. They called her "Sleeping Beauty." Hospital bills mounted to over $600,000, and insurance coverage was terminated.

What brought Tiffany out of the coma? Pam Delaney sat next to her daughter's bedside day after day. She began to recall memories of Tiffany and Sabrina when they were both little girls. Pam and Larry had taught them when they were little that if they ever got frightened in a public place to run over and grab their mom and dad's hands and squeeze three times.

Both parents would then return three squeezes without saying a word. That message meant "I Love You."

So while Tiffany was struggling to stay alive, Pam Delaney etched out a touching poem about Tiffany. She quoted to her there in that hospital bed:

• • •

A brief life curtained, dreams of no use
Tears that overwhelm for a shattered youth

Her eyes once sparkled — now they're dimmed with pain
A voice that was eager lives in silent domain
Intelligence and beauty — they once were her own
The light now is shrouded like a spent candle blown
A childhood memory that long ceased to be
A game that was played by the children and me
Whenever afraid or alone or unsure
They would take Mom or Dad's hand,
holding firm and secure
Three little squeezes — that was the game
As I sit and I watch her I still play the game
I hold on to her hand and whisper her name
I don't know if I can reach her — I pray I get through
Please, Tiffany, don't you remember
Three squeezes mean I love you?

. . .

Several months later, Tiffany came out of her coma! Who can underestimate the power of embracing your son or daughter? The *San Fernando Daily News* headline boldly proclaimed, "Crash Victim Defies Prognosis." The article read, "After ten months in a hospital bed — half of that time spent in a coma — nineteen-year-old Tiffany Delaney motioned her mother to her bedside. 'I love you, Mom,' she said. They were her first intelligible words since January 27" (December 10, 1989).

Sister Sabrina also went through much trauma. She had a ruptured spleen, and her arms and legs were broken in several places. She has also recuperated.

Tiffany is walking now. She is talking. A miracle that reminds every parent to embrace their kids.

. . .

Chapter 8

. . .

Follow Me...You'll Be OK
Step #7 — Model the Message!

This is the simple *"Do as I do,"* not the *"do as I say"* approach. Your kids respond to you every day, whether you know it or not. "I hear what you say. I see what you do."

. . .

*Kids may doubt what you say, but
they will always believe what you do.*
— The Bible Friend

. . .

Kids mirror their parents. They reflect their parents' attitudes, prejudices, and convictions. Statistically, it is proven that there is a significant percentage of young people who adopt their parents' poor parenting skills and abuse of drugs or alcohol. They even inflict physical and sexual abuse on others *if* they received the same from their parents.

Modeling is crucial in saving our kids from ruin. You can be assured that your children will mimic you. What are they seeing as they view your life? What values are you holding up in front of them? Is your faith viable enough for them to follow? Is your commitment authentic? What about your loyalty to your spouse? How is your sexual behavior? What kind of language do you use with your kids? Don't come down on them for imitating your behavior in life.

. . .

Six most important words to model:
"I admit I made a mistake."

. . .

Count on it—they will follow your example, whether good or bad. I have met those rare young people who rose above the pitiful standard that their parents had set for them. Somehow, they sprouted wings and flew above it. Most often, however, that is not the case.

Sometimes I get exasperated with poor parental models who could care less about the damaging impact they have on the young lives in their care. I know someday they will be responsible, but in the here and now the damage on a young life is incalculable.

. . .

Five most important words:
"You did a good job."

. . .

A Great Model Parent Named "Norman"

How would you as a parent feel if someone wished the worst thing on one of your children, and it actually came true? For NFL Jets quarterback, Boomer Esiason, and his wife Cheryl, this horrible wish came true six years after the birth of their first child, a son by the name of Gunnar.

It was all a terrible mistake! With the NFL on strike in the fall of 1987, Boomer had been instrumental in leading his teammates against management. After a long Sunday afternoon of severe criticism outside the Riverfront Stadium in Cincinnati, Boomer jumped into his car with Cheryl and headed home. Listening to the radio seemed to be the only

▲ JERRY WITH HIS WIFE CHRISTIE,
DAUGHTERS DANIELLE AND JENILEE, AND SON, JEREMY.

DAN DOELL DIED ▶
OF AIDS ON
FEBRUARY 10, 1994.

▼ SANDY YEAROUT WAS SPARED
FROM RUIN BECAUSE OF HER
PARENTS TEX AND PEGGY.

KEN WHITMIRE PHOTOGRAPHY

◄ NFL QUARTERBACK,
BOOMER ESIASON,
WHAT A DAD!

GEORGE AND LINDA ►
GLEASON WITH AMY.

▲ JERRY JOHNSTON HAS APPEARED ON
520 RADIO AND TELEVISION PROGRAMS.

▲ OVER 4 MILLION YOUNG PEOPLE HAVE HEARD JERRY
ON 3,200 PUBLIC HIGH SCHOOL CAMPUSES.

deterrent from such a hostile day, when all at once, some of the local sports talk shows announced that Boomer had pretty much arranged for the Bengals' wives to boycott an event they had organized that would benefit the Cincinnati Children's Hospital because of the strike.

Radio callers were violent and agitated. The allegations against Boomer were not true. Anyone who really knew him knew he gave an incredible amount of time to charity in both a public and private way—none so touching as the trips he made to the Children's Hospital to visit kids fighting leukemia and cystic fibrosis.

By this time, Boomer and Cheryl were listening with indignation. Suddenly, a man's voice came over the air to cast his wish upon the Esiasons with all of Cincinnati listening. "You know what I hope?" thundered the man. "I hope the Esiasons have a child that has something wrong with it someday, and Children's Hospital turns them away."

"That's unspeakable," said Cheryl. The pain and hurt from the man's statement would resurface six years later when in a hospital room a doctor would confirm that their little blond haired, two-year-old Gunnar had cystic fibrosis. This is a deadly disease that clogs the lungs with bacteria-trapping phlegm and shuts off the work of the pancreas, making it impossible for the body to absorb most foods.

"We are sorry, Gunnar. We love you" were the only words Boomer and Cheryl could muster as the precious boy lay asleep with tubes in his arms and nose.

As Boomer left the hospital that day, on the way home a flood of emotions overcame this strong athlete. Remembering back to his childhood experience with his father, Norman, Boomer decided that little Gunnar would become his life just like he had been Norman's.

Since age six, Boomer was raised by his forty-four-year-old father after his mother, Irene, lost a six-month battle with lymphoma. "Boomer" was a nickname his mother had affectionately given to him because of the kicks he had delivered inside her belly, and it would be the name he would carry with him to the NFL someday. Only now would Boomer begin to treasure the precious childhood memories with his father, Norman, at the head of every major event in his life.

Through those first few lonely years after Irene's death, Norman would race home to watch young Boomer play football, baseball, and basketball. He never missed a game, even though he had a one-hour-and-ten-minute train commute to and from his job each day. This little boy became Norman's life.

They played catch and watched the New York Mets and New York Rangers together while sprawled out on the sofa, with Boomer lying right on top of his dad's chest—a pose that would later become familiar to Boomer and little Gunnar after his intense twenty-minute therapy on a sloped vinyl board.

When Boomer was a young boy, the Esiason's house was the center for all his friends to spend the night and partake of Norman's jelly crepes the following morning for breakfast. At least three or four friends would accompany Boomer on his summer vacations. His surroundings were so full of love and happiness that when it came time for him to leave home because of a scholarship to the University of Maryland, needless to say, it was a frightening experience.

Everything was different for Boomer at college. He was a seventh stringer in a very strange place and flunking half of his classes. All his friends at school would be free to go home on weekends and have their moms do their laundry and cook dinner. This created a silence within his heart. He was about to give up, throw in the towel, and go home when during practice he noticed Norman sitting in a lawn chair, stiff from the five-hour drive. That wonderful, friendly face that had been there for him time and time again had rescued him once more.

Boomer's love for people, "all people," grew greater in the years to come. He became big without running over the small. He had made a name for himself in the NFL, but privately he gave most of the credit to that wonderful man, Norman. Cheryl would tease Boomer on occasion that he never really grew up. The doorbell would ring and the neighbor kids would ask if Boomer "could come out to play?" as if he were still eight years old.

Finally, in April of 1991, it was time for Boomer and Cheryl to have one of their own, a "Boomer baby." Cheryl had decided to give their little one a nickname too, but it would be just the opposite of the one Irene had given to her baby. Boomer's life was a busy one, and Cheryl was bound and determined that their child would not get swept up in the whirlwind of it all; thus came the nickname, "Baby Sub Rosa," which means private, confidential, secret, in Latin. Life seemed to be as perfect as could be for the Esiasons; an NFL career going great guns and a happy home life with a new baby added to all the present blessings. At the height of this bliss came destruction.

Little Gunnar kept getting sick with persistent colds, diarrhea, pneumonia, and lack of appetite. At first, the doctors diagnosed his illness as asthma. He couldn't sleep or breathe. Many nights at 4 A.M. Boomer would take little Gunnar and drive around Riverfront Stadium trying to get him to fall asleep. In March of 1993, Cheryl took Gunnar back to Children's Hospital because of recurring pneumonia. At this point, the doctors retested him for cystic fibrosis. Their worst nightmare had now become reality. The Esiasons' blissful world was now being turned upside down. Their future would be a campaign full of fundraisers to help fight cystic fibrosis and a myriad of morning talk shows. Good-bye "Baby Sub Rosa." Hello CF poster child.

Boomer became determined that he would be the biggest enemy this disease had ever had. In the back of his mind, Boomer would recall all the fond memories he had as a child; the little boy whose mother died when he was only six and the father who would be there throughout all the hurt. Norman never had to say who you had to be for your children or how much of your life you would have to give away for them. He just lived it every day right before Boomer's very eyes. Now when it was all said and done, Boomer was the father of the little boy with cystic fibrosis (story adapted from "We're Going to Beat This Thing," by Gary Smith, *Sports Illustrated,* Oct. 4, 1993, p. 18).

Proper modeling can do wonders for any son or daughter. Begin your modeling process today!

. . .

Chapter 9

. . .

We Care, Amy

Step #8—Care Enough to Correct!

Correcting our kids is not an easy assignment. When I discipline our children, Christie cringes, and I cringe when she does. We are working our way through this whole thing as is every parent.

One thing for sure, every child needs the security of a parent who cares enough to do something about disobedience! By standing between our children and their poor decisions saying, "I will not let you destroy your life," we prove to them that we care.

. . .

Everything else in the modern home
is controlled with the flick of a switch.
Why not the children?

. . .

1. Be Honest with Your Discipline

As parents, it is easy to go overboard or underboard with our discipline. This is very confusing to our children. It is crucial that we become honest with our children as we correct them. Tell them exactly what you are doing and why you are correcting them.

2. Be Consistent with Your Discipline

Perhaps most confusing to children is when a parent responds to improper actions one day and lets it go by the next. Establish your boundaries and the convictions you and your family are going to live by. Then, don't back down! Your kids, like mine, will test you. They will say, "I hear what Dad says, but let's see if he really means it."

Be consistent! Your consistency establishes in your children's mind a value system of right and wrong. Our prisons are full of inmates where that code of behavior was not clearly defined to them in their formative years.

3. Don't Discipline in Anger

This is tough! When your child does something that is wrong, it is easy to explode. Wait! Do not administer correction when you are angered. Tell them, "After dinner, we'll handle this," or "When we get home, meet me in the family room."

America's most common, but least reported crime, is domestic violence. Some of that violence is at the hands of an angry parent administering *punishment* instead of *correction*. There is a difference.

4. Discipline with Love

When God deals with us, He deals with us in love. The spanking ought to hurt the parent far more than the child. After correction, every mom and dad should hug their son or daughter, tell them repeatedly, "I love you, and that is why I am doing this." Let them feel your love. Initially, they may hate you. Down deep they will know you truly care. The parent who does not respond to disobedience is the one who genuinely *does not* care.

5. Discipline Privately

There is nothing more humiliating to a child than to be corrected in front of friends, family members, and especially in a public place! Never, never, do that. Get alone with your son or daughter before any correction is administered.

6. Communicate with Your Discipline

Some parents correct their children but barely say a word. "My dad gets really quiet when he is mad. I don't know what I did. He is really mad," one teen said after his father disciplined him.

What good is correction like that? Tell your children:

(1) What they did wrong.

(2) How they violated the rule.

(3) Why you are correcting them and how.

(4) Reaffirm to them that your love for them is the motivation for the correction.

(5) Tell them to expect your consistent response if they continue to disobey.

7. Model the Behavior You Want Them to Imitate

Every child's first role model should be their dad and mom. In our topsy-turvy world, that is often not the case. Make it the case in your home. When you blow it, admit it to your kids. If you have a problem or an addiction, tell them. Don't pretend. I promise you, kids identify more perfectly with imperfect, flawed, honest parents than with perfect dishonest ones.

. . .

*It is easier to build boys and girls
than repair men and women*

. . .

George and Linda Gleason

George and Linda Gleason are two parents who used great wisdom in saving their daughter Amy from ruin at a pivotal time in her life. Every parent in America needs to hear their unique story.

After speaking to and counseling with over 4 million kids all across North America, I soon learned not to be overly affected or moved by the stories I was being told by kids and their parents. I must admit, however, that last October was not one of those times.

Two months earlier, I had been invited to speak to a group in Ozark, Arkansas. I must honestly say that after traveling to some of the more beautiful spots in our great country, Ozark had little appeal to me, and there was little anticipation in my spirit about the trip.

After arriving in Arkansas, I was told I would be dining in the home of George and Linda Gleason. George Gleason owned several banks in Arkansas and had previously served with the Rose Law Firm in Little Rock with a now famous partner by the name of Hillary Clinton. He and Linda have four children: a daughter Amy and three sons, Eric, Tripp, and Peter.

My speaking engagement went very well that night, and before leaving, I invited George and Linda to travel to Kansas City and allow my wife and me to return the favor and have dinner with us. They graciously accepted, and eight weeks later we found ourselves at a downtown restaurant enjoying the food as well as each other's company. Since I had been with the Gleasons on a previous occasion, I felt somewhat more familiar with them than did my wife, Christie. However, halfway through dinner, all that would change.

I felt a bit sorry for Christie as she tried to finish her meal, restrain the tears, and listen to George as he told the most incredible heart-wrenching story we had heard in a long time.

Our hearts melted in their presence as George dove deeper and deeper into their yearlong saga. Christie would take short, quick glances over toward Linda to see if tears were swelling up in Linda's brown eyes. I imagine she didn't want to feel alone at the table as the one and only Kleenex she had was wet and terribly overused.

George honestly confessed to us that eighteen months earlier, their sixteen-year-old daughter, Amy, admitted to them that she was pregnant. He and Linda had just returned from a business trip. They were tired and worn enough from the traveling without this news that seemed at the time almost too much to bear.

As George began to divulge more and more of the intricate details of Amy's story, it was pretty obvious the hurt and pain they had endured was resurfacing.

Tension filled Amy's bedroom as first she told Linda and then George of the pregnancy. Neither one was prepared for such a life-changing revelation. Amy was crying from a combination of fear and shame. Linda was stunned and devastated. George searched to make some sense of the situation.

Getting no answers from Amy, George decided it was best for him to leave the room. He found a quiet place in their bedroom and did the only thing that came natural at a time like this. He prayed! In seconds his anger faded as God reminded him of certain promises such as Romans 9:28 and James 1:2-4. George claimed God's promise that even this would work together for good in the Gleason household and that even this trial could be counted as joy.

The months that followed tested the Gleason family's

faith in those promises. It was hard to see much good in the situation. Joy was hard to hold onto in the midst of such trials.

Amy seemed, for a time, to be genuinely repentant. She even seemed to understand when George and Linda forbade her to see the non-Christian boy who had impregnated her. Amy knew she was dependent on the help of her parents, particularly with the coming baby, so she tried to get along.

But less than two months after the initial revelation, the Gleasons received another blow. Amy miscarried. George described it this way. "We had just adjusted to the idea of having a baby in the household and then the baby died."

The miscarriage brought with it a very unwelcome change in Amy's attitude. No longer did she sense her need for her parents so much. She became very rebellious and wanted to return to her old lifestyle and relationships. The Gleasons were locked in a battle for their daughter's future and her soul. It was a battle they were determined to win no matter what the cost.

Several more weeks passed with growing conflict. Amy grew more rebellious and determined to get her way. George and Linda dug in, determined to prevent their daughter from going against God's will and ruining her life. The situation finally exploded one night in July when Amy was caught lying about her plans for the evening. That night George searched his daughter's room, read her diary, and discovered the truth—Amy's life had gotten far more off course than he or Linda had ever imagined.

When the big confrontation came, Amy fully rebelled, threatening to run away and marry the non-Christian boyfriend. A battle raged in her bedroom. About to be overcome by anger, George left the room and went to his own room to pray. Within thirty minutes God brought to mind Scriptures and revealed to George a plan to save his daughter. Exhausted and thankful for the insight, George fell in bed and went to sleep.

As far as George knew, Linda was still upstairs trying to reason with her wayward daughter. But unknown to George, she had left Amy's room just a few minutes later and was on her knees with God in the den. Linda would end up spending most of the night there in steadfast prayer.

When George awoke the next morning, he got out of bed without waking Linda, showered, and got ready to go to work. As he was getting dressed, Linda awoke and came into the bathroom. He promptly announced that God had given him an answer to the situation.

Without even waiting for a response from Linda, George jumped into the explanation. He said they must totally separate Amy from this boy and her other friends who were encouraging her rebellion. He explained that Linda would move to Little Rock (two hours away), rent a house, enroll Amy in a Christian school, and Linda would devote the next year of her life to trying to restore and disciple Amy.

Linda put her arms around George as her tears ran down his chest. George was sure such a bold plan and the prospect of being apart for a year had broken Linda's heart. She hugged her husband tightly and said, "I prayed for three hours last night in the den and God gave me the exact same answer. I just didn't know how I was going to tell you."

In the next few days, George and Linda continued in earnest prayer and study of God's Word, reconfirming what God had revealed to each of them as they prayed in separate rooms that night. They knew they would have to take dramatic measures such as these for Amy to have any chance of getting her life and mind straight.

It was important for Amy to be taken out of her present surroundings, away from the young man who impregnated her, who obviously did not love her, and away from the friends they felt were dragging her down. Mostly, George and Linda just knew it was imperative for Amy and her mother to have this time alone; time to rebuild their relationship and to try to restore Amy's commitment to God.

This would be a difficult time for the entire family. George would take on the role of a single father during the next year. He remained in Ozark with the boys while Linda and Amy headed for Little Rock almost two hours away.

The couple who had been inseparable must now settle for a casual wave as they passed one another at the designated mile-marker on I-40 or twice weekly as they shared a few hours together at the office.

George and Linda concluded that it was imperative that Amy never be left alone until she had established herself in her new environment and could be trusted again. It was agreed that Linda would retain her job at the bank in Ozark and on Mondays, after dropping Amy off at her new Christian school, she would make the two hour jaunt back to Ozark. George, on the other hand, would leave Ozark in time to pick Amy up from school. On Tuesdays, the roles would reverse and each would head the opposite direction.

It was a challenging schedule. Linda got to spend very little time with the boys and George got to spend very little time with Amy. Workdays were shortened by the continuous travel adding to the stress. But the entire family knew this was God's plan and was committed to see it through. That is, everyone except Amy.

The truth of the matter is, Amy thought her parents were "nuts" for moving her away. This was the last thing she wanted and she made her feelings on the subject well known. She threatened to run away on several occasions and became increasingly hostile toward both parents as the move approached and even for months afterward.

George and Linda clung to the assurance that God had given them this plan. As the months passed away, Amy's resistance and rebellion began to soften. Linda and Amy began to make big steps in restoring their relationship to what it had once been. Despite Amy's predisposition to hate her new school and not make any new friends, she soon had many new friends including a new Christian boyfriend. On a date one night, this spiritually sensitive young man named Andy began to talk with Amy about her faith and her life. As they talked Amy was convicted that her prior salvation decision was not genuine and that night she prayed to receive Jesus Christ. From that day forward, Amy's outlook and life began to change quickly.

Amy would walk away from that year in Little Rock with one very important change in her life. She had a profound spiritual experience and a totally new outlook on life.

By the time George had concluded this very riveting story, we were all oblivious to the fact that the restaurant was now empty and the waiters were looking at us as if to say, "How much longer can this man talk?" I know Christie had to be as wrung out as I was. You can't hear a story like this one and just ask, "What's for dessert?"

Sitting there with two total strangers, we felt as if we had known each other for years. Funny how parents can feel such instant kinship through sharing tales of their children.

I can't leave you hanging without sharing the epilogue of the story. Amy is now eighteen and in her first year at a fine Christian college. She is planning to return there next year to begin her sophomore year. Even as I write this book, the Gleasons are vacationing together. "TOGETHER" being the key word.

Perhaps the best ending to this story is told in Amy's own words. Amy included this special note in her mother's birthday card toward the end of what may have been the Gleason family's longest year.

> I just wanted to say I love you! It has finally hit me that in three months I will be gone. I'm sorry for not spending as much time with you as I should have. I love you so much and appreciate very much what you have done for me. For one thing—you gave me a second chance in life—and I turned it into something special. That's probably one of the best things you could have done for me. It has made our relationship stronger and I now have a special relationship with the Lord. I just

wanted to say Happy Birthday and Thank You! You're a very special mom and don't you ever think differently! (OK?)

Thank God for happy endings to a very troubled situation!

Chapter 10

I've Got a Dream
Step #9—Nurture the Dream!

Did you know that hidden somewhere within your child there is a dream? They have a goal of becoming someone in life. To save our kids from ruin, we must **NURTURE THE DREAM** within our kids. Take the time to discover the dream within your son or daughter. Help it come out in them, and together paint a picture of what they can become.

Discovering the dream begins with ten questions every child should ask their own parents. Every mom or dad should answer these questions honestly, giving their response to their children. In addition, you cannot nurture the dream if you do not have open, active communication with your children.

Dream Development Questions

Questions Kids Must Ask Their Parents
(Mom and Dad, or Mom or Dad if a Single Parent)

1. Do you love me? Really love me? Describe your love for me.

2. Are you my friend?

3. Do you *care enough* about me to forgive me if I fail at

some personal things in life, such as drugs, alcohol, and school grades?

4. If I make a mistake or appear slow or stupid, will you not make fun of me or belittle me?

5. Will you be *real* and genuine around me and not phony? Will you tell me how it really is?

6. Will you "not act like a kid" around my friends? Also, will you not act like a stuffed shirt around my friends? Just act like a normal, natural parent of your age.

7. Do you realize that I will take on many of your characteristics? Will you tell me specifically the ones that you would rather I didn't adopt? And will you change those specific ones in your life as an example of good faith to me?

8. If my career choice in life is not what you *dream* for me, will you accept it anyway, with enthusiasm for me, and not try to change me? Will you help me develop my dream?

9. Will you *trust* me? Don't build a fence around me all my life that has no gates.

10. Will you *not* treat me like I was a kid all my life. Accept me as I am at my age and back off with your lectures, criticisms, and questions. Just realize that the prerequisite for perfection for a kid is to have a *perfect parent*, and you aren't one. But I love you anyway, just as you love me in the same way—as I am.

Kids and parents should grade themselves and each other by allowing ten points for a yes and zero points for a no. Five points is given for "yes—so-so."

Score Results

90–100	You are near-perfect
70–89	You are extraordinary
50–69	You are good
30–49	You need to improve
0–29	You need HELP

Weighty questions, indeed. Each one deserves your most serious consideration.

. . .

Socrates said, "Could I climb to the highest place in Athens, I would lift my voice and proclaim—fellow citizens, why do ye turn and scrape every stone together for wealth, and take so little care of your children to whom one day you must relinquish it all?

. . .

The following individuals made their mark on the world. Some were inspired correctly, some incorrectly; regardless, each one had a dream. As you read the following stories, let them motivate you so that, as Ronald Reagan's father quipped when he was a boy in poverty, "Who knows, maybe someday you will grow up and be the President." It happened. The *Dream Developer* in Ronald Reagan's life was his mother, a godly, wonderful Christian.

They Had a Dream

Pete Maravich

The day was June 22, 1947, and Press Maravich, a professional basketball player in his own right, was on top of the world. His wife had just delivered a precious baby boy, and Press was elated to say the least.

"We're calling this boy Peter Press Maravich, Doc! Remember that name," he said. (Pete Maravich and Darrell Campbell, *Pistol Pete: Heir to a Dream*, Nashville: Thomas Nelson Publishers).

Press' words rang true that day, but the doctor wouldn't be the only one who would remember little Pete's name. America would remember him as the most prolific scorer in college basketball history, averaging 44.2 points during his years at LSU.

Pete went on to have a highly successful ten-year NBA career in which he was selected twice to the All-Star team and was the youngest man ever elected to the Basketball Hall of Fame.

Many of us, however, simply remember him as "Pistol Pete" or "The Pistol" — a name that was given to him in the eighth grade by a newspaper reporter who, during a pregame warm-up, told Pete he looked like he was drawing a pistol when he launched the ball. Pete's fellow teammates overheard this passing comment, and the nickname "Pistol Pete" stuck. "Pistol Pete" was a memorable sight on the court with his forever shaggy hair and white floppy socks.

After Pete's death in January 1988, I recalled the first time Pete and I met. I was at a speaking engagement in the South, and it wasn't really expected to be anything out of the ordinary. During the prelude, my host that day leaned over to me and said, "Jerry, do you see who is sitting out in the audience tonight?" Sorry to say that without my glasses on, I could barely see past the third row of seats. "It's 'Pistol Pete' Maravich and his father, Press," he said.

I was ecstatic! I had heard of this man's achievement for several years and counted it a privilege to have him in my meeting that night.

When I finished speaking, Pete and his father made their way through the crowd to speak with me. That night marked the beginning of a short three-year friendship with a man I still feel was the most sincere, genuine, and warm-hearted person I had ever known.

A few months later, I was booked to speak at another meeting and was told I would be sharing the platform with Pete Maravich. Through a series of events, Pete and I got together and decided to collaborate our efforts and do several meetings together.

I had no idea that Pete was such a health enthusiast. The first time he showed up at our home, my poor wife needed to be totally disarmed. We offered Pete root beer on the rocks and Snickers bars as an after dinner snack; thus began Pete's mission for my family. He was obsessed to say the least. During the next few years, whenever we would reunite on the road, Pete would emphasize to us our need to "come clean" and give up all those unhealthy foods. My dear wife would graciously listen to his speeches and relinquish her rights for junk food by the time Pete got through with her.

"This is an intense man," my wife would often say. He had a passion for the things he believed in and an even greater desire to see people adhere to his way of thinking. People often labeled him as "a misunderstood genius."

What was behind this extraordinary intellect and to what did he credit all his success?

Anybody who knew Pete would know that his father wanted to nurture Pete since birth to attain to greater things than he had. Besides being a coach to hundreds of players, Press saw it as his mission in life to properly coach little Pete. There was a strategy behind everything he did for Pete. Press saw Pete's need for serious instruction and would invent a method of teaching that would later be called, "Homework Basketball." This is when the legend of Pete Maravich truly began — childhood stories of a little boy who was totally obsessed with the game of basketball. He would lie in bed at night and shoot the ball to the ceiling and catch it, all the while repeating, "fingertip control, backspin, follow-through." Pete would then sharpen his skills by dribbling the ball on his two-mile walks to town, alternating hands to become equally adept with both. He was known to regularly dribble the ball while riding a bicycle and would commonly sit on the aisle seat in the movie theater so he could dribble throughout the show. As Press would drive the family car, at altering speeds, Pete would hang out the window and dribble. He had become a basketball android.

As the years went on, Pete would feel so close to his dad in the study of the game that Press began treating Pete as if he were an assistant coach.

In February 1974, after his fourth year as an NBA player, Pete was interviewed by sportswriter Andy Nuzzo who was with a paper in Beaver, Pennsylvania. During the interview, Pete said, "I don't want to play ten years in the NBA and die of a heart attack at age forty."

That statement became a reality in 1988 when, on January 5, "Pistol Pete" Maravich died of a rare congenital heart condition at age forty.

. . .

Big shots are small shots
who keep on shooting!

. . .

Steven Jobs

In the 1970s, the world would be transformed with the introduction of the Apple Computer. It was not one man, but two who were behind such a machine that would leave its mark on history.

Steven Wozniak invented the first Apple personal computer (PC), but it was Steven Jobs who would become surrogate father, nurturing the PC concept to fruition. Jobs, age twenty, sold his Volkswagen bus, and Wozniak, age twenty-four, sold his HP calculator for $1,300 to raise the much needed money to build the first units of the Apple 1.

Steven Jobs defied all the odds put against him. He was an orphan who was later adopted by Paul and Clara Jobs. Growing up in the '60s, he courted rebellion, the nonconformity that symbolized the era. He was considered a rebel and a loner during his high school years. He had spent his life thus far searching for meaning and a desire to know his real parents. Steven was looking for an identity within the establishment culture. Being the perfectionist he was, Steven had a compulsive drive to achieve power. He was in constant search of his "blissful oblivion."

His family became Apple. He had nothing else. It would be his only identity at this point. Steven Jobs was successful because he believed.

Regis McKenna, a press agent with Apple Computer in the early days, would give a statement to the crucial role Steven Jobs played in the development of the PC: "I don't deny that Steven Wozniak designed a good machine. But, that machine would be sitting in hobby shops today were it not for Steven Jobs. Woz was fortunate to hook up with an evangelist" (Gene N. Landrum, *Profiles of a Genius*, 75).

. . .

If you want a place in the sun,
you have to expect some blisters.

. . .

Tom Monaghan

Tom Monaghan was brought into the world on March 25, 1937 in Ann Arbor, Michigan. After his father's death in 1944, Tom would be transported from one foster home to the next. Before the first grade, he had lived in several orphanages, thus culminating his childhood with unhappy and unsettled events. As a youngster, he spent many hours reading and dreaming of better days. For six and one-half years, he lived at St. Joseph's Home for Boys, a Catholic orphanage in Michigan, which he often referred to as a prison, and he felt his fellow classmates were inmates.

In his adolescence, he became enamored with great leaders such as Lincoln, P.T. Barnum, and Frank Lloyd Wright, because of their ability to rise from poor beginnings to wealth and fame. Tom would make it his wish to try to equal these men he had now taken on as his heroes.

When Tom turned eleven his mother brought his younger brother home to live with her, and he was left in boarding school. Tom was devastated to say the least. Eventually, his mother did bring him home. However, it was too late. Family clash and conflict resulted, forcing Tom to leave home. He enlisted in the Marine Corps in 1956 and credits that experience in his life for his zeal for discipline and fitness.

At twenty-three, Tom purchased DomiNick in Ypsilanti, Michigan with his brother. After only a year in business, he convinced his brother to release his interest in the business, and they sealed the deal after Tom gave him his used Volkswagen Beetle. Four years later, Tom renamed his business Domino's and started operating stores near college campuses. But he wouldn't stop there. He was forever looking to the future, always dreaming. He would continually be guilty of "leaping before looking." He would go on to create the world's largest pizza delivery chain based on simplicity and efficiency. He totally refused to offer sandwiches or any other product that would distract his store managers from the main objective of delivering the best pizza in the fastest time. Tom Monaghan is a very religious man and credits his success to a higher power, God!

He once told his wife that he would be a millionaire by the time he reached thirty years of age. He has always believed in himself, in other people, in God, and in hot, fast, tasty, home-delivered pizzas (Adapted from *Profiles of a Genius*).

These people were nudged to nurture their dream in their lives. Nurture it in your own children. Inseparable to the dream your child possesses is the realization that they have *super self-value.* Let's look at that in the next chapter.

. . .

*The secret of success is to do
the common things uncommonly well.*
—*John D. Rockefeller, Jr.*

. . .

Chapter 11

I'm Ready, I've Got an Answer
Step #10 — Teach Prepared Reaction Responses!

Why is it our kids can recite a television jingle in a split second, but they draw a total blank when one of their "friends" is pressuring them to try drugs? It is very simple: They have not **PREPARED THEIR REACTION RESPONSE** in advance. This requires an insightful parent's leadership.

To save your kids from ruin, it is imperative that you help them develop their **Prepared Reaction Response** (PRR) to those crucial events and times in their lives when the decisions they make will determine the future of their lives. These climactic events and times in their lives will assuredly come, as we have seen in the stories in this book, and will determine their well-being.

Your son's or daughter's response must not be one to be considered, or thought out, or debated at the moment of decision with the other person involved. It *must* be PRE (before) considered, carefully thought out, debated, and decided long before the event and time.

The **Prepared Reaction Response** cannot be pressured or coerced on your child. Instead, it must be openly discussed, measured, weighed, and talked about at great lengths. The responder must consider all the pros and cons of each respective decision. It must be dialogued between the parent and child, not just an insisted monologue of the parent's views.

The **Prepared Reaction Response** must be spoken to and

about on your child's level, not the intellectual level of the parent. It must be nonemotional and factual to the point where your child completely understands all of the ramifications and elements of the proposed decision. It cannot be made up of clichés and trite sayings.

Of necessity, some of the points of discussion regarding potential decisions will be sensitive, subjective, tender, and personal.

As parents, we need to view children's development similar to them walking through a minefield. One wrong step, one wrong decision, can destroy their life. I believe we must teach our kids three vital areas regarding their personal lives and the decisions they will make. They are:

1. **RESPECT.** Our children must respect themselves. They should never succumb to the idea that they are not vitally important. They should never be bullied by some friend or harassed by some individual wanting to exploit them. Again, this is where the parent comes in. We need to tell them every day, "**You are great. There is no one like you. Your future is fabulous. You are number one.**" Through the years, I have noticed whenever kids lose respect for themselves, they totally bomb out. Respect is the glue that holds a kid together.

2. **CONTROL.** Our children must stay in control of their lives at all times and in all circumstances. Drugs and alcohol are two things that will take them out of control. Sex can make them slaves. In my mind, this goes back to the parent. Are you modeling any behavior before them that indicates you are out of control? If you are, expect the same in their lives. Kids must understand the dangers of drugs, alcohol, and anything else where they can experience an addiction. This is our job as parents. Teach your children to always be in control of their lives. We stay in control by maintaining a set of personal disciplines. Every child should be

taught that there are certain things you say no to. Make it very clear to them.

3. **OBEDIENCE.** Don't be afraid to enforce obedience with your children but always discipline with love. We do our children great harm when we don't discipline them. Every kid needs the security of knowing he or she has a parent who cares enough to do something about disobedience. Lay the law down! Give them the rules! When they violate them, respond. Do it because you love them.

Recently, I spoke at a military academy. What a unique assembly it was. They marched all the cadets in, and you could have heard a pin drop. Once they were all in place, no one moved. They dared not sit down in their chairs until the order was given. Each cadet was looking straight ahead. They barely blinked an eye. The order was given, and they sat down and relaxed.

Many parents who won't discipline their kids send them to a military academy like this one to make their children obey. It costs $11,000 a year. I know a more inexpensive way. Begin when they are young. Let them know who is boss. Don't be a coward with your kids.

The **Prepared Reaction Response** is simple: I will say no to a negative, damaging, destructive, illegal, immoral request. I will say yes to a positive, constructive, edifying, mature, legal, moral request.

The **Prepared Reaction Response** is not one of consideration, thought, or debate at the time. It is a pure, plain, simple, uncompromising *no* to the negative, and a *yes* to the positive.

Set the Stage with Your Child

Sit down with your children and propose the hypothetical situations they will be in during their growing years, and together *write down* their **Prepared Reaction Response** to some of the different temptations that will be proposed to them. (For the purpose of illustration, we will use the name Julie.)

1. Hey, Julie, will you do drugs with me?

PRR No, I don't want the weight of an addiction in my life. (Write down your own **Prepared Reaction Response**)

2. Hey, Julie, let's rip this sweater off from the mall. C'mon, lets do it. Will you take it?

PRR No, I'm not going to get arrested. That's stupid.

3. Hey, Julie, let's have sex. Will you? I love you.

PRR No, if you really loved me, you wouldn't be pressuring me to have sex. Forget it.

4. Hey, Julie, will you go out drinking with me tonight?

PRR No, I don't want to vomit. I'm happy sober.

5. Hey, Julie, let's stay out all night, OK?

PRR No, come on over and spend the evening at my house. It's a lot more comfortable and fun over here.

6. Hey, Julie, let's buy a *Playgirl* magazine. Will you buy it for us?

PRR No, I don't want my eyes contaminated!

7. Hey, Julie, let's take the car out and race. Will you drive?

PRR   No, I've seen the pictures of kids' bodies that look like they have gone through a meat grinder. I like my body the way it is now.

8.   Hey, Julie, let's go tear up Chris' house. You throw the first brick, will you?

PRR   No, the cops can outrun me.

Some of these **Prepared Reaction Responses** sound a little corny, but they are better than you ignoring the fact that every temptation possible will be posed to your son or daughter. Sit down now with your kids and plan their responses together in advance. Then they will be ready when the question and situation comes along.

The **Prepared Reaction Response** will certainly have its reward with your son or daughter. It means:

> No to drugs and no addiction.
> No to stealing and no arrests.
> No to sex and no STD's, AIDS, or guilt.
> No to booze and no illness, addiction, and damaging decisions.
> No to bad memories, personal handicaps, and injuring or killing a friend.
> No to the possibility of being confined in a locked room.

I have met those brilliant students who are leaders and who know how to stand up to their friends. In almost every case, as I quizzed them on how and why they were prepared to face their peers, they responded that their parents had helped them develop their resolve.

Parents, help your children develop their own **Prepared Reaction Response** to every situation they will find themselves. You will sleep a lot better when they are out on a Friday or Saturday night. Do it today.

. . .

Chapter 12

. . .

You're the Greatest!
Step #11 — Instill Super Self-value!

How do we instill value into our children? We transmit value into our children. Their value is perceived by our explanation to them on how vitally important they are. Your child is a unique, special gift! You can instill value in them in several ways:

1. Help Them Identify Their Personal Gifts and Talents

All children have innate skills God has given to them. As parents, we must assist our children in identifying the gifts they possess. We do this by letting them attempt different activities and athletic events. Furthermore, we must cut them some slack so they can try different interests.

2. Play with Them

No one should play harder or have any more fun with your children than you. Why play with them? By playing with them, you will get to know them. You are going to see their strengths and weaknesses. Moreover, your laughing together and having fun together will weld you together.

Do you have fun with your kids? If not, start now.

3. Stick with Them through Their Problems

As many of the stories in this book testify, kids can make it through their problems if their parents stick with them. Don't abandon them in the middle of their problems. Stay right in there helping them work their way through it all. They will never forget it.

By all means, don't keep throwing their errors in their face. When they have failed, forgive them and forget it! Don't hound them. Don't become their personal priest and demand a repeated confession every time the memory of their failure comes before you.

4. Assist Them in Setting and Reaching Goals

All children have a dream to become something when properly motivated by their parents. Help your children set their personal goals. Work with your children until the goals are met.

One of the best ways is to write their goals down together and put a nonpressure timeline with it. When they succeed, praise them. When they fail, *praise them* as well.

5. Don't Demand Perfection

I meet parents all the time who live out their dreams through their children. It is such a sad sight! These parents push and push and push their kids until they break. Some children, instead of breaking, turn to drugs or alcohol or become violent. Demand the best, not perfection.

A Pastor's Wife Who Slit Her Throat

What would you say about a minister's wife who got so desperate with her life and whose self-value was so low, that one night she tried to commit suicide? Meet Les Raymond, wife of Pastor Don Raymond.

While speaking at Bell Hall on the world famous Fort Leavenworth United States Military Base in Leavenworth, Kansas, Don Raymond presided as the chairman of our united effort in the community. I was extremely impressed with what a genuine person he was. One day while eating lunch with him and his wife, I noticed a scar across his wife's throat. She seemed like such a perfect pastor's wife. Since her scar intrigued me, Don shared with me quite openly and honestly that his wife, Les, slit her throat one night in desperation.

The problem stemmed back to Les' childhood with her parents who were, of all things, missionaries. The following is a question and answer session I conducted with Don and Les Raymond. It is shocking to read and certainly reminds every parent the absolute crucial responsibility of **INSTILLING SUPER SELF-VALUE** in our children.

JJ: I want you to tell us a little about your ministry, your background, and how you met.

Don: I've been in the ministry for about twenty-five years, and we've been in our present ministry for almost six years. Les and I met in her freshmen year and my sophomore year in college. We dated that year, and that next summer we were married.

JJ: Les, you're right now just finishing work to be a registered nurse. That's pretty significant, considering everything you've been through. Tell me about your background — your family.

Les: My parents were missionaries on the island of Jamaica for ten years, and then they taught at a Bible college. Also my dad preached and my mom taught kindergarten. They both have written books. They were just totally involved in all types of Christian work.

JJ: And you were raised in Jamaica?

Les: That was my childhood.

JJ: I want to try to re-create the story of what you went through. Go ahead and tell us. You had some physical complications that very fateful night when you almost lost your life.

Les: There were so many factors that led up to that, but at the time I can only remember feeling as if I wanted to run away from my life. Having been raised in such a strong Christian home and having the role of minister's wife set before me, and feeling disillusioned at not being able to live that role, and seeing inconsistencies of what I dreamed the church and ministry should be, all those things compiled together to make me feel unfulfilled and unhappy. I was always searching, whether it was in relationships or getting a job. I was running and searching for something to make me feel fulfilled and happy. And while all this was going on, our marriage was going downhill. We weren't communicating. We were both very active serving the Lord, but not taking the time to work on our own relationship. In fact, on the surface I may have seemed at the time to be the ideal minister's wife because that's all that showed. I kept everything inside. Yet inside, I felt as if I were dying. Actually, the night that I tried to take my own life was the end of about five years of running from the Lord and running from myself.

I finally decided that life wasn't worth living. Of course, we had talked about my physical illness. At the time, however, we didn't know that I had lupus, but I was always fighting this feeling of sickness and always going to one doctor after another doctor and being told there was nothing wrong with me. All this culminated in my decision that life wasn't worth living; that Christianity was not what it was cracked up to be; that life, no matter what you did, you weren't going to be happy or fulfilled, and that happiness was not to be found. So I decided to take my own life.

That particular night, I waited until my husband was out of town. In fact, he was at camp, and the children were visiting their grandparents. At 2 in the morning, I got a razor blade and I cut my throat. I was a little bit frightened. I wanted to do it so quickly that I wouldn't have a chance to change my mind. I was a little afraid that I might change my mind, which is why I decided to get into the car and start driving. I thought that driving would keep my hands on the wheel and keep my mind on the road so that I wouldn't change my mind during the few minutes that it would take. Little did I know that God had other plans for me that night.

JJ: Re-create that night for us. You were on a very small town road, going from Topeka to Manhattan.

Les: Lawrence.

JJ: What highway is that?

Don: Highway 24 from Topeka to Lawrence.

JJ: It's the middle of the night.

Les: Two in the morning.

JJ: The oddity of the license check that inadvertently saved your life. Can you bring all that back for us?

Les: The thing that moves my heart, even this many years in looking back, is something a little newspaper article revealed. Someone later sent us this article, written by a reporter who interviewed the chief of police of Lawrence, asking him why they had called a license check at 2 in the morning on a highway like 24, which wasn't traveled on much at night. They weren't trying to catch anyone in particular. In fact, the chief had no explanation for his actions. Since he couldn't sleep, he got out of bed at 2 in the morning and called a license check. His action saved my life. And that's the same time, 2 in the morning, when I cut my throat and began to drive down that highway. I remember seeing the blinking red lights ahead and not knowing what it was. I hit the brakes, and the last thing I remember seeing was a police officer jumping out of the way of my car.

JJ: You obviously didn't stop.

Les: I didn't stop the car. Later I was told that when my foot came off the accelerator, the officer ran after the car and was able to catch it before it went into a ditch. He got me to the hospital in time, and the doctor said it was close.

JJ: This story impacts me so much because I am thinking, here's a pastor's wife who tried to kill herself and the incredible slim margin of anyone who slits their throat making it. I mean, there's a lot of easier ways to terminate yourself than that. You'd been married five years. You have two children.

Don: At that time, we'd been married eight years. But I think at that same time, we were very much caught up in the mentality in which both Les and I had been brought up. And that was that we were to serve the Lord. I can remember bragging to other ministers that I hadn't been home for one night in six weeks. I was out serving the Lord, and at that time, we had two preschool kids. This left a lot of responsibility for Les. I was out calling and working with the youth, and the week that this took place, I was at a senior high week at Bible camp. And they had to call me to come down to the hospital to see Les.

JJ: What did you think, Don, when you found out your wife had gotten so desperate that she had tried to kill herself?

Don: Well, my first thought was, and I think this goes back to where I was mentally, *Why would she do a thing like this?* You know, here she had two lovely kids, a husband who was faithful, and a ministry that was growing in Topeka. What more could she want? So why would she do such a thing like this? I was really out of touch with where she was mentally at that time, while she was looking for me to give her emotional help, encouragement, and time with her. And I simply wasn't in tune to her. It wasn't that I was purposely trying to be negligent. It was just negligence out of, I think now, stupidity, because my focus wasn't on my marriage and my wife. My focus was on serving the Lord and winning souls for God's kingdom, and giving all my time to kingdom work.

JJ: Now, Les, after you recuperated, things didn't get better. In fact, they got worse. Can you pick up the story?

Les: Yes, it's because there had been no change in my heart. I was no sooner back home from the hospital when the next crisis came up. It was a small crisis — just a small argument between my husband and me, but that's all it took. This time I can remember actually thinking and saying to the Lord, "OK, God, if You won't let me kill myself" . . . you see, I recognized that God must have intervened. But I did not see that —

JJ: Even in a state of rebellion?

Les: Yes, I recognized that there had to be intervention. It was just too many coincidences. But I still said to God, "If You won't let me kill myself, I'll just run away, and You can't stop me." This is where I had gotten to in my rebellion toward God. So I just packed my bags and left. I parked my car in front of a laundromat and hired a taxi to take me to the bus station. I didn't want them to be able to trace my car to the bus station. I took a bus to Kansas City, and I spent a few nights in roach-infested hotels, looking through the newspaper for a job. I finally got a job as a cocktail waitress in a hotel bar.

JJ. Where were your mom and dad, I mean, did you ever feel inclined to call them during any of this period and say, "You've got to help me—I'm going down"?

Les: That's a good question, Jerry. No, I didn't. It wasn't because I didn't love my parents, but there's something I think is important to touch on here. My parents, with every good intention, always strove to teach us that the Christian life was one as near perfection as you could get. My perception of my mother was someone who was near perfect, and I could never attain to that level of perfection. I didn't feel I could ever achieve what she desired for me. I would never have purposely invited their disdain. I just never considered that what I was doing would personally hurt them. I was looking from a selfish perspective. I was more afraid of getting their disdain.

JJ: In this hotel in Kansas City, as a cocktail waitress, you must have felt horrible. You had children; your husband was a pastor; and yet the motivation was your emptiness. How did it come to an end?

Les: Jerry, it's like you said; the thought of what I had been all my life and now where I was—where my own running and selfishness had brought me—hit me hard. But the turning point was when I was changing hotel rooms, moving into a hotel where I was working, which was a fancy hotel. As I was unpacking my things in my room, I opened the top dresser drawer, and there was a Gideon Bible. To me, that was like a slap in the face because one of the important things my parents had done for me as a child was teach me to memorize Scripture. I had already memorized five books of the Bible and thousands of other verses. I knew what I was doing was wrong. I knew that I was running from God, and to be confronted with a Bible at that point was like a slap in the face.

I slammed the drawer and said some ugly things about the Gideons and about God's Word. When I heard myself say those things, it just all hit me, and I burst into tears and cried for three hours straight. I got down on my knees by the side of the bed and just cried. During that time of crying, I really feel that the Spirit was pleading on my behalf. When I got to the end of those three hours of tears, I realized that if I was going to make a decision to turn to God, I needed to do it then or I might never desire to do so.

Jerry, that scared me to death because I was reserving that right to someday return to God. I didn't want to throw God out entirely. I just wanted to live this portion of my life the way I wanted, and to think that I might lose that desire scared me. I then saw that I was at the bottom of the barrel. So I stood up and literally held out my hands, saying, "OK, God. I'm giving all of me to You, and make of my life whatever You want. I'll do whatever You ask. I'll be whatever You want. Whatever You do, please don't let me get this far away from You ever again." I knew, Jerry, at that time God wanted me to go home to be with my husband; that He wanted me to reconcile. I did not want to, but I had made a conscious decision that no matter what, I was going to be obedient to God.

I picked up the phone and called home. That was a very difficult thing. Don answered, and I told him I wanted to come home. He wasn't so sure that he wanted me to come home because for five years, I had been in and out. He never knew when I was going to be at home. Now that I had packed my bags and left this time, he wasn't sure. Then, he did say, "You can come home as long as you will meet with me and the elders, tell them what you've done, and ask for their help and guidance." And I hung up on him. For that split second, my reaction was no. I will not do that, and I had to turn around and call again because the decision I had made to God was so strong that I realized that I had said, **"No matter what, I'm going to do what God wants me to do."** For me, that was the turning point.

JJ: And from everything I understand, Don, that was the turning point.

Don: Yes, it really was. For several years preceding that event, every time there was a crisis, every time she'd get upset, she'd get into the car and leave. She might be gone a day or a night, and during this time our kids were still in preschool. I think Dan was in kindergarten at this time. I had the responsibility, and they were wondering where Mommy was, but I didn't know where Mommy was. They were getting to the age when they were beginning to ask questions, and it was beginning to affect them. I felt the time had come. I had never seriously thought about divorcing Les, but I knew I couldn't continue with what was happening in our home and in our marriage—having her here today and gone tomorrow and not knowing where she was. I did say to her, "Don't come home again. Don't use any of the charge cards because I've changed the names. You can't write any checks on our account. Don't come home unless, if you do come home, you're home to stay, and we're going to work this thing out."

A few days later she called from the bus station and said, "I'm home." Then things began to change for us. We both began to work on our marriage. I didn't see it any longer as Les' problem. It was *our* problem. We were a husband and wife, and I had to change some attitudes. I had to change some priorities and some values in our home. So I had to become a different type of husband. I had to begin to work on that and study and read and go to seminars—marriage seminars—on how I could be a better husband and a better father. And Les began to do some things. All these things began to bring about a change in our marriage. We literally learned to love each other and fall in love with each other. I can still remember those days when I'd look at couples and say, "Man, I'd give anything to have a marriage like they have." And the Lord fulfilled that desire for Les and me.

JJ: You know, Les, it's just amazing that a missionary's kid could go that far away from the Lord. I know this may be painful, but I know there's a word that is reverberating in everyone's mind—Why? I ask because we've got an innumerable amount of parents who seem to have ideal families across America and you seem to have been raised in a similar environment, but they're losing their sons and daughters. Many of them don't know their kids are sexually active or doing drugs or drinking or are involved in things that would blow their minds. But this is happening. It happened right under your parents' eyes. What were the reasons? Why?

Les: That's a hard question to answer. I know some of the pieces of the answer. For example, one of the things that used to be strongly taught—and it wasn't taught just by my parents, a whole generation was taught this, and we were actually repeating it as small kids—was that service to God involved only those things outside the home, such as going to church and doing Christian activities. Service to God wasn't your relationship with your family. Don and I have since learned that that's not true. Our relationship with God begins with our relationship with our family and then extends outward.

However, my parents had been strongly taught that commitment to the Lord means to be involved outside the home in whatever ministry God gave them. They didn't realize that being totally uninvolved in their children's lives was going to create emotional havoc for us. The fact that they were uninvolved in our lives created an emotional disaster (there's four of us—I have a brother and two sisters). And we've talked about the tremendous emotional turmoil we all felt. Yet it was not anything that my parents did on purpose. They didn't decide to ignore their children and not go to any of our school events. It was just the mind-set that was taught back then.

JJ: What things did your parents not attend that you wished they had?

Les: Every event that I was in at school. In fact, the one event that my mother did attend was when my grandmother came to town and insisted on seeing a school activity that I was in, but then my grandmother was appalled at a little burlesque dance some of the school kids did on stage. In fact, she wrote a letter to the newspaper, blasting the school for allowing that. My one event that my mother came to caused the whole school to laugh at me because my grandmother wrote a letter to the newspaper. My father never did come to anything.

JJ: Did he ever say why he couldn't come?

Les: They were always too busy serving the Lord. I can remember my mother saying, "Honey, these things will not count when it comes to eternity." So she didn't see it as neglect. She saw these things as being trivial. These were temporal things. Since these weren't things that will count for eternity, I shouldn't have my heart in them. Yet, as children, because that was our life at the time, we didn't see them as trivial. They were mammothly important to us. When our parents weren't involved in our lives, it created tremendous emotional turmoil. And yet, Jerry, I turned around and did the same thing when my kids were small. I was so involved in my life, fulfilling the role that I thought a minister's wife was supposed to fill, that I was totally uninvolved in their lives.

JJ: Don, how do you relate to this? You've gone through therapy sessions with Les.

Don: You know, you asked Les the question, "What are some of the things your parents didn't attend?" These weren't minor things that her parents didn't go to. For example, they didn't go to her high school graduation.

JJ: Why?

Les: I don't think they saw it as a major event.

JJ: Graduating from high school?

Don: It was an expected event. Les was a straight "A" student. Straight "A" students graduate from high school and then they go on to college. She was in an orchestra, and they never heard her play. She was crowned queen at one of her school events. They never saw her crowned queen. It's not just school events. As Les grew up as a little girl, she never sat on her dad's lap. She was never hugged. She didn't have that physical relationship with her father that a girl or any child needs. Only discipline was there in the home.

JJ: Now, define that physical relationship that you're referring to. Plenty of hugs?

Don: Hugs and affirmation; sitting on Daddy's lap; being told how important you are; how you are loved; how meaningful you are to your parent—just all that personal affirmation and encouragement that a child desperately needs. Les didn't receive any of that. In talking to her mom since that time, her mom's feelings were that Les didn't need it. She was a well-rounded little girl. Since she was a good girl at school, she didn't need it.

JJ: She was smart. She knew where she was going.

Don: And yet I think this lack of physical affection from her father played a very important role in our dating relationship and even our early married years. Les desired a lot of physical attention from me, while I

147

wasn't aware of some of these things that had happened to her. I wasn't aware of a husband's responsibility to do these things. So there was the real need that she had and my lack of awareness of even doing some things that a husband should be doing — giving personal affirmation and those kind of things. I was busy trying to support her and doing the things that I thought were important. I overlooked a lot of the emotional things. So this really added to her emotional crisis.

JJ: How did your parents respond when they found out you had attempted suicide?

Les: I didn't find out until much later what their response was. My mom later said that she just cried and that Daddy just held her as she cried. And I need to remark that just in the past five years my relationship with my mother and father has taken a totally different turn. Before that, however, my mother was totally unaware of the tremendous emotional impact that not having affirmation as a child had upon me, that I was always seeking to get her approval. I can remember in grade school when I came home with half A's and half B's, and my mom said to me, "Well, that's nice honey. Pretty soon you'll be getting straight A's." What that said to me was "Great honey, but it's not good enough." The message I remember from my childhood, which was said in many different ways for many years, was "Good job, honey, but not good enough." I always felt that I was never quite good enough, and she didn't realize that I was always striving for that affirmation.

Now my older sister, who really struggled emotionally with self-esteem, made it quite known to Mom and Dad that she needed affirmation. So they gave her affirmation freely and openly. They were always saying, "Oh, Nita, what a beautiful poem you've written." Yet they didn't see that I also had that need. So I went totally unaffirmed. But in the last five years it's changed. It's never too late.

My parents are now great-grandparents, and they have totally changed their relationship to me. My mom will now affirm my talents. She will take every opportunity that she can to build me up in a valid way, not flattery, but in a valid way. Even my dad has remarked, "You know, honey, I was just not taught the importance of hugging and physical love and touch. I was just aware that I had three young ladies and that I should treat them as young ladies. I didn't realize that I should have you on my lap and hug you."

JJ: Were they involved in the therapy sessions when you were putting your life back together?

Don: Yes, on one occasion, when they were living in New Mexico, they came to Topeka and went through some of the therapy sessions with us. In fact, there were some sessions where there was just Les and her dad. At that time, the therapist really enlightened Les' dad of her need and what was happening. That was part of the change.

You know, we mentioned that after coming back from Kansas City, some changes began to take place. Well, that was part of the change. Les and I received counseling, and we brought our parents into it. We looked at her early years of childhood and how these things affected her and how they were affecting her presently. That began the reconciliation process, which included forgiveness and dealing with bitterness. These things had to be dealt with.

JJ: If they don't get dealt with . . .

Don: There's no change. Change comes as a result of recognizing the problem, admitting it, confessing it on both parts, and then beginning to bring about reconciliation. Reconciliation means that now Les' mom treats her differently and gives her recognition and approval. That's changed behavior and that's vitally important if there's going to be change taking place.

JJ: What do you want to say to parents?

Les: That it's not too late. You can't go back and undo what's been done. You can't change what's past, but you can change your future. It's never too late to start treating your kids with respect. Treat them like they're important people. Don't speak to them rudely, even if you have to discipline them or correct them. Do it with respect. Recognize their accomplishments. Focus on what they do right and what they do well. Don't focus on where they don't meet your expectations, because the emotional trauma that will be passed on to them and their children and their children's children just snowballs.

Don: I'm thankful that Les and I went through these things when our kids were young. As they went into Little League and then into junior high and high school sports, I can tell you today that when my daughter was playing sports in junior high and high school, I attended every game, even if it meant missing an elders' meeting, even if it meant traveling out of town. At that time, we were in Minnesota, and I went all over the state of Minnesota to watch her run races and play basketball, and she knew that she was important to me. I think it's vital that we who are in the people business begin to recognize that our family is people and they're a part of our congregation. We need to go out of the way to help our own family, just as we go out of the way to help a family in the congregation. It's a shame that many times we have time for every family in our church except for the family that calls us Dad and Mom.

JJ: You are both intelligent people. How has it changed you as parents, that is, what you went through?

Les: My first response is that it hasn't changed me enough because I still have that tendency to want to strive for perfection. But, Jerry, it's changed my life immeasurably. As far as the memories that my children have, it's interesting that the first time my daughter learned what I went through was when I invited her to attend a Gideon banquet.

JJ: Fill us in on what you've done with Gideons. I think that's important.

Les: I happened to share my testimony of that Gideon Bible in that hotel room with a Gideon. Within two weeks, I received a phone call to share my testimony at a Gideon Banquet. At that banquet, I received seven invitations from pastors to come to their churches. Basically, the Gideons then opened the door for what became a ten-year, full-time, speaking and singing ministry, which also included recording and writing music.

But as I was speaking at a Gideon Banquet, I decided to invite my daughter who, at that time, was either in junior high or in high school. She had never heard my story. She later said to me, "Mom, what a way to do it! You invited me. I'm sitting there in front at a table with everybody looking at me and hearing this about my mother for the first time." But, Jerry, you've mentioned to me before that part of making a ministry valid is to be transparent. I determined that what I had been through needed to become a part of my ministry and that I could no longer hide it. For a long time I tried to hide it. But when you've got a scar on your neck, people wonder if you've had an operation or whatever. Yet there are ways to hide it. So when I decided to make everything I'd been through a part of my ministry to people and be transparent, that included my children. We had to involve them and say, "Kids, here's what we put you through. You might have been too young to remember it at the time, but we need to ask for *your* forgiveness for the rough years that you had as children." I had to ask forgiveness of my children for being in and out of the home for five years. Basically, the stability of their father kept the home together.

I think we learned too that our children are a priority in our lives. Now they're both married and out of the home, but they were and still are a real priority. Family vacations, family time, family events, birthdays, and Christmas were special times in our home, and we really tried to make Dan and Cindy feel special and wanted and needed. Those were changes that we made, and we really went overboard on some of these things. I remember when Cindy turned sixteen, we decorated the whole house and put all kinds of things on the wall that really said this was a special time in her life. I think our kids really responded well to that. They knew that Mom and Dad loved them.

What a story! Les Raymond is a vibrant testimony. Thank God, she is still alive. Her story reminds each one of us of the need to **INSTILL SUPER SELF-VALUE** in our kids.

Chapter 13

I Wasn't Able
to Handle the Pressure
Step #12—Enforce "Just Say Wait!"

Mary, a tenth-grader, said, "I wasn't able to handle the pressure. I was a part of a group in junior high that was into partying, hanging out, and drinking. I started to have sex with my boyfriend, and it was a real downer. It was totally against what I was, but it was important to be a part of the group. Everybody was doing it."

Sharon, a senior, added, "I'd say half the girls in my graduating class are virgins, but you won't believe those freshmen and sophomores. By the time they graduate, there aren't going to be any virgins left."

It's nothing new to any parent who surveys the sexual habits of young people in a sex-soaked culture where expressions of erotica seem to be everywhere. Kids are having sex today at younger ages than ever before. It seems like almost everybody is "doing it."

"Kids are continuing to try sex at an ever more tender age: more than a third of fifteen-year-old boys have had sexual intercourse, as have 27 percent of fifteen-year-old girls—up from 19 percent in 1982. Among sexually active teenage girls, 61 percent have had multiple partners, up from 38 percent in 1971. Among boys, incidents like the score-keeping Spur-Posse gang in California and the sexual-assault convictions of the Glen Ridge, New Jersey, jock stars suggest that whatever is being taught, responsible sexuality isn't being learned" (Nancy Gibbs, "How Should We Teach

Our Children about Sex?" *Time*, May 24, 1993, 61).

Experts offer a raft of reasons why they believe peer pressure among teenagers is one of the most important reasons for taking the sexual plunge. One Atlanta teen said, "If you say no, you're a tease, and if you say yes, you're a slut."

A professor at Ohio State University, who has studied teenage sexuality for more than a decade, sees a slide in moral values. It isn't a big deal to be a virgin today. It's not one of those high-value items. It is simply a question of teenagers not seeing anything wrong with it. They see it on TV and in books. Sexuality is so prevalent that it is just assumed that it is a form of self-expression.

One mother said, "Deep down I know it is going to happen sometime, no matter what I say. Is my oldest daughter a virgin? I don't really know, and the tough part is that I really don't want to know."

This mother expressed the sentiment of many of today's parents. However, it is crucial in saving your child from ruin that you talk explicitly and directly regarding sex. Kids are crying out for their parents to talk specifically about this issue.

Why? Because kids are bombarded with sex in our society today. Young people see it everywhere in movies, commercials, magazines, and ads that sell everything from cars to soap. Sex sells, any way you look at it. Sex tantalizes. Sex excites. Sex attracts. But now in the 1990s, sex can also kill. Sex can leave you diseased, scarred, lonely, and suffering.

. . .

It's a strange life.
You can skate on thin ice
and end up in hot water.

. . .

In the popular movie, *Indecent Proposal*, starring Woody Harrelson as David, a down-on-his-luck architect, Demi

Moore as Diana, his wife, and Robert Redford as John Gage, the smooth-as-dice billionaire, Gage offers David a million dollars to sleep with his wife for one night. This film comes from sexual-sensation director Adrian Lyne, who also directed the popular movies *9 1/2 Weeks* and *Fatal Attraction.*

For his signature sex scenes, Lyne used handheld cameras to make the audiences think they're spying on the actual act, and he lighted the bodies so that they appeared to glow from within. In *Indecent Proposal,* he suggested that even a fantasy wife might welcome an excuse a lot less tempting than a million dollars to get in bed with someone new. Lyne believes the whole idea of monogamy is hypocrisy.

This is the prevailing attitude of our day. "Almost one third of all married Americans (31 percent) have had or are now having an affair. This isn't a number from Hollywood or New York City. It's the national average for adultery. Today, the majority of Americans (62 percent) think that there's nothing morally wrong with the affairs they're having. Once again, we hear the killer rationalization that 'everybody else does it too' " (James Patterson and Peter Kim, *The Day America Told The Truth* [New York: Prentice Hall Press, 1991], 94–95).

I know it comes as a big surprise to many entertainment celebrities, but there are still millions of God-fearing people who are not betraying their marital vows. These parents who have kids *must* give them the reasons to **JUST SAY WAIT!** Sex is great in its right context, and only in its right context: MARRIAGE. One man for one woman for one lifetime!

· · ·

You can find the world's shortest sermon
on a thousand traffic signs:
"Keep right."
—Amarillo News

· · ·

There are many experiences in life. We attempt to remember the best of them in the form of photo albums. How we relish those memories! There is one memory in life every person never forgets: the first time, place, and person they had sex with. Why? Because as God intended, sex is a very sacred gift He has given to every man and woman.

Give Your Kids a Reason to "Just Say Wait" to Sex Until Marriage

Yes, I believe kids will wait to have sex if we are responsible and informative enough to give them what I like to call "The Advantages of Abstinence." Mark the following eight "Advantages of Abstinence." Share them with your son or daughter, and give them plenty of opportunity to respond to every point. They may have questions or comments. Give them an opportunity to respond.

Advantage #1—Avoid Sexually Transmitted Diseases

It is very simple to understand. All of this freewheeling sexual experimentation by so many has caused twenty-one lethal sexually transmitted diseases to be active and potentially deadly among those who determine to express themselves sexually. Abstinence is the only approach that guarantees absolute protection from these harmful diseases transmitted so easily through sexual activity.

The Center for Disease Control reports that an adolescent contracts an STD every thirty seconds in the United States. One in four sexually active teens will contract an STD. Syphilis is at its highest level in forty years, and gonorrhea is America's most commonly reported communicable disease. The Alan Guttmacher Institute report shows that 25 percent of Americans will contract an STD at some point in their lives. That is one out of every four people in our nation!

As has been widely reported, condoms are not "safe sex." One study reports condoms fail one out of every six times they are used. Scores of wives with sexually experienced husbands still get pregnant every day because the condoms broke or something went wrong. Adjusting to an unexpected pregnancy in marriage is totally different however, than a teen getting pregnant or getting a disease that has no known cure.

Researchers have pointed out that unbroken latex gloves have had "channels" of five microns size, which penetrated the entire thickness of glove. Meanwhile, the HIV measures .1 microns and is 1/25 the width of sperm.

Explain carefully the deadliness of having sex with someone who may be infected. Kevin Irvine, for instance, began having unprotected sex at age sixteen—the same year he learned he had been infected with the AIDS virus through blood treatments for his hemophilia. His girlfriend didn't know about his infection. She said, "I'm on the pill, so we don't need to use condoms." After he found out about the AIDS virus it was impossible to go back, he said, without telling the girl he'd put her at risk. Later, he took the same risks with a second girlfriend. (Kim Painter, "Atoning for Reckless Errors of Youth," *USA Today*, June 3, 1993, 6D).

Advantage #2—Avoid Suicidal Thoughts and Depression

Our personhood, sense of self-respect, and self-worth are directly linked to our sexuality. If you don't think that is true, ask a prostitute how she feels about herself.

Several studies conducted by medical doctors have corroborated that a high percentage of sexually active young females develop suicidal thoughts after they participate in sex. These same sexually active young people are also more likely to have drug and alcohol problems than their non-sexually active peers.

Doctors Adcock, Nagy, and Simpson studied 3,803 students, grades eight through ten for stress, depression, and attempted suicide. They were examined by gender, ethnicity, locale (urban vs. rural), participation in sexual intercourse, and the use of alcohol. They found the following: Females were at greater risk than males. Both males and females who engaged in sexual intercourse and alcohol consumption were at greater risk than were abstainers. White adolescents who engaged in these behaviors were at significantly greater risk than were those who abstained.

Doctors Orr, Beiter, and Ingersoll, after studying 1,504 junior high students (twelve to sixteen years of age), found nonvirginal boys and girls were significantly more likely than their virginal peers to engage in other activities considered risky. Nonvirginal boys and girls were also at significantly greater risk in engaging in minor delinquent acts and having school problems. Nonvirginal girls (but not boys) were 6.3 times more likely to report having attempted suicide. Nonvirginal girls were at slightly greater risk for reporting feeling lonely, feeling upset, and having difficulty sleeping. A significant proportion of the students reported having sexual experience and using alcohol or marijuana (45 percent boys and 27 percent girls).

Explain to your son and/or daughter that sexual expression is a very serious behavior intended only for marriage.

Advantage #3—Avoid Unwanted, Ill-timed Pregnancy

Getting pregnant is great—when you are married! Before marriage, however, pregnancy can cause devastating problems for a young girl and her boyfriend (read Amy Gleason's story in chap. 9).

Over 1 million unmarried girls get pregnant each year in America. A documented 400,000 plus will get an abortion annually—sad and tragic. The emotional upheaval thrust upon a young girl has never been told in terms of statistics. Most of these single-parent families are living at the poverty level.

Advantage #4 — Realize the Honor of Marriage

Early sex detracts from long-term relationships. Moreover, sexual activity prior to marriage dishonors and denigrates the office of marriage.

No thinking person wants a short-term marriage. Contrary to widespread opinion, divorce has had a profound effect on kids. A National Center for Health Statistics study revealed children from single-parent homes were 100 percent to 200 percent more likely to have emotional or behavioral problems and about 50 percent more likely to have learning disabilities. In the nation's hospitals, over 80 percent of adolescents admitted for psychiatric reasons come from single-parent families.

Advantage #5 — Avoid the Emotional Scars of Being "Used"

As I speak all over the world, and as young people come to me, I observe how unhappy they are. Much of their unhappiness stems from "experiencing too much too soon." Nowhere is this more glaring than in the sexual arena. To many guys, sex is "conquest." To a girl, it most often is "commitment." A girl gives herself to a guy because she thinks it will seal a relationship. She is proving the degree of her commitment. But when a guy gets what he wants or gets tired of the same piece of flesh, he's off to another girl.

Sure, girls dump guys. However, I have seen a lot more girls who have been dumped than guys. There is no pain to a girl like the feeling of being "used."

. . .

> *All the water in the world,*
> *However hard it tried,*
> *Could never sink a ship*
> *unless it got inside.*
>
> *All the evil in the world,*
> *The wickedness and sin,*

Can never sink the soul's craft
Unless it got inside.

. . .

You can avoid all of that by saving yourself for the special person God is reserving for you. The greatest gift you can give your mate on your wedding night is not a ring; it is you! There will be no regret on waiting for the right person at the right time.

Because many kids come from dysfunctional families in this turbulent decade, at times their sexual expression is not just a biological urge. In some respects, it can be a knee-jerk reaction to some lack or need in their own life. Expressing themselves sexually, with all the inherent physical and emotional dangers, only compounds the problem.

Advantage #6 — Experience the Thrill of Sex As It Was Created

Some people think Christians or devout Jews are prudish. They have missed the point! Only a true believer can experience the thrilling dynamics of sex as God originally intended it.

In the Old Testament there is a very unique, smaller book entitled, *The Song of Songs*. It is nothing more than a manual of the depths of physical love. Did you know a Jewish boy was not allowed to read this book until the age of fifteen? It is supercharged with the ecstasy of inexhaustible physical love between two who have the genuine bond of love between them.

To God, sex is not dirty. It is not just for procreation. Sex is for joy—a tool to love with, saying, "I love you, and you alone!"

By saving yourself, you will experience the thrill of sex as God intended.

Advantage #7 — Experience Long-term Love

In a speaking engagement I recently had in the Cayman Islands, they honored a couple who had been married seventy-five years!

You cannot love someone if you do not know them. To really get to know someone takes time. Genuine love is totally different from the erotica we see on the silver screen or on television. The best sex is in a long-term relationship encircled with love.

Advantage #8—Your Prize of Virginity

If a girl or guy stays pure, chances are they will be ridiculed. In our society, we are making virginity seem like social leprosy with all of our sex accommodation. I think, in a sense, it is good for a young person to be ridiculed. It weeds out those who are really standing for their convictions from those who are just paying lip service.

Don't ever forget, teen, that while your friends are ridiculing you for being a virgin, deep down they respect you. Deep down they are saying to themselves, "I wish I could be like her or him." Look at your purity as a prize. Don't give it to anyone except the mate God has prepared just for you.

Much press attention has been devoted to the True Love Waits Campaign that my own denomination has enacted across America. It is a brilliant program. Thousands of kids all over America are making a pledge to stay pure until marriage. They are signing a card that reads, "BELIEVING THAT TRUE LOVE WAITS, I MAKE A COMMITMENT TO GOD, MYSELF, MY FAMILY, THOSE I DATE, MY FUTURE MATE, AND MY FUTURE CHILDREN TO BE SEXUALLY PURE UNTIL THE DAY I ENTER A COVENANT MARRIAGE RELATIONSHIP."

. . .

There was a Scotchman who had a dress shirt which he wore on special occasions. After he had used it several times, he would question its cleanness and take it to the window for

better light. His wife's words were very wise:
"If it's doubtful, it's dirty."
　　　　　　— V. Raymond Edman

. . .

The True Love Waits Campaign received its biggest boost to date when the nation's largest denomination, the fifty-nine-million-member Roman Catholic Church, came on board. The National Federation for Catholic Youth Ministry plans to send 180 dioceses literature discussing adolescent sexuality, including modified chastity pledge cards for Catholic young people. Church officials say the gathering together of some of the nation's largest denominations for the program may herald a new sexual revolution among teens and help convince government policy-makers of the value of teaching abstinence to prevent disease and teenage pregnancy.

I am so excited about this campaign! There are ten "Behavior Guidelines" that govern this program for teens:

1. I will date only Christian guys or gals.
2. I will seek my parent's counsel (or another spiritual authority) before consenting to date another person.
3. I will understand my standards before I agree to date.
4. I will either plan out or be sure that each date is planned out.
5. I will not put myself or my date in a position to defend his or her right to be pure.
6. I will build up the spiritual, intellectual, and emotional before the physical.
7. I will not be left alone at home with my dating partner.
8. I will not engage in petting or intimate physical contact.

9. I will not lie down with my dating partner.
10. I will not engage in premarital sex.

Parents must address the sexual area with their children early to save them from ruin. There are plenty of good reasons to wait to have sex until marriage. Many a child has become a "casualty in life" because of failure in this one area. Don't let it happen to your children. Let's look at the next step.

Chapter 14

It's a Violent Home

*Step #13—Protect Them—Virtue,
Not Violence, in Your Home!*

Can a gang member kill your son or daughter? Yes. Can violence in the next year, two years, or beyond victimize your family? There is a very strong possibility. Will your child become an object of violence before he or she graduates from high school? Let's hope not. Yet the facts paint a scary picture.

My organization recently produced a shocking video entitled, "Kids and Gangs." It was recently aired on prime time TV nationwide. The response was significant. With the help of experts, I defined the reasons why a gang member will kill any person. It is going to surprise you. Here they are:

1. If he thinks you disrespect him.
2. Just for the heck of it.
3. As a random initiation requirement.
4. If you are presumed to be his enemy.
5. Because you said something wrong.
6. So he can feel powerful in his area.
7. If you look at him funny.
8. If you give him a mean look.
9. Because he doesn't like the way you look.
10. Wearing the wrong colors.
11. For your money, your car, your jewelry.
12. If he thinks you have drugs.
13. Because he thinks you disgraced him.

14. Because you touched him.
15. Because you resist his advances.
16. Because you smile at his advances.
17. If you fight him.
18. If he thinks you are a spy.
19. If you walk a certain way.
20. If he wants something and you resist him.
21. If you joke with him.
22. If he doesn't like your attitude.
23. If he is high on drugs.
24. If he is drunk.
25. Just horsing around.
26. If you snitch on him.
27. If, as a woman, you deny his request.
28. If you are ugly in any way.
29. If you damage his car.
30. If his gang tells him to.

These Are the Reasons a Gang Member Will Kill You!

Violence among the young is so rampant that the American Academy of Pediatrics calls it a national public health emergency. Among fifteen- to nineteen-year-olds, homicide by firearms is the second-leading cause of death (after motor vehicle crashes) for whites and the leading cause of death for blacks.

Where is the concentration of the most severe violence in America? This is going to shock you . . . the home! It is not in some darkened alley. In fact, it may be in that nice house next to yours with the perfectly manicured lawn, or it may even be in your own home.

Fortune magazine devoted one issue to a special report entitled, "Children in Crisis: The Struggle to Save America's Kids," which presented some grim findings. Consider the trends:

For too many children, there are no safe havens. They are victimized at home at school, on the street. An astonishing number of youngsters are beaten, maimed, molested, and murdered by parents, relatives, or baby-sitters. The National Committee for the Prevention of Child Abuse (NCPCA), using reports filed by all 50 states, calculates that 2.7 million kids—some 4 percent of American children—suffered from abuse or neglect last year.

Among older children, the numbers are even bleaker. More adolescents die from violence—especially gun violence—than from any illness. According to the National Center for Health Statistics, homicide by firearms is now the second-leading cause of death (after motor vehicle crashes) for 15-19-year old whites. For African-Americans in that age bracket, homicide is the leading cause of death.

Teenage violence mostly affects urban African-Americans (except for suicide, a predominantly white problem). But it is beginning to spread. Under pressure from big city police departments, gangs are stashing their guns and dope in the suburbs and recruiting high school students as pushers. . . . The most pressing task is to get guns away from children. The widespread availability of firearms makes it far too easy for kids to kill and be killed. Guns figure in more than 75 percent of adolescent suicides. Should we really be surprised that so many children are infatuated with firearms? There are more than 200 million privately owned guns in America, and half of all households have at least one. A five-year study by the American Psychological Association found that the average child has witnessed 8,000 murders and 100,000 other acts of violence on television by the time he or she has completed sixth grade" (Ronald Henkoff, *"Kids Are Killing, Dying, Bleeding,"* **Fortune Magazine**, *August 10, 1992, 63).*

The United States is an increasingly violent country. The Center for Disease Control reports that 2.5 million teens carry guns, knives, razors, or clubs to school. Up to 135,000 guns are carried into the schools *each* day. Now one fourth of the nation's schools have installed metal detectors in the entrances. More school districts are signing up for metal detectors because they cannot curb the violent behavior of the young people in their respective schools.

When I was preparing to speak at a high school in Indianapolis, Indiana, the principal abruptly stopped my assembly. She leaned over and said to me away from the microphone, "I'm sorry, Jerry, we are shaking down the campus for guns with a SWAT team." I remember sliding back in my seat thinking *what in the world has happened to America.*

One student came up after my assembly and requested to talk with one of our counselors. This young teen had been very moved by what he had just heard. He confessed to the counselor that he had been involved in five murders!

This is not just an inner-city/ghetto problem. The middle-to upper-class suburbs are also experiencing their woes in youth violence. In my own community, one student planted a bomb, which exploded in the bathroom. Thank God, no students were hurt. It could have killed many.

Throughout the nation, there is not a week during the school year when violence associated with guns does not affect U.S. public school campuses.

USA TODAY monitored one recent school year, September to June, and compiled a chronology, which sounds like a war zone of some anarchistic country:

> SEPT. 7–11: AMARILLO, TX. A seventeen-year-old student opens fire in a Palo Duro High School hallway with a .38-caliber pistol, wounding six students. A seventh student is trampled in the panic.
>
> SEPT. 14–18: JACKSONVILLE, FL. A fourteen-year-old student shoots his tenth-grade girlfriend in the

back at Englewood High School. He surrenders moments later with a small-caliber semiautomatic pistol.

SEPT. 21–25: ROCHESTER, NY. A seventeen-year-old student shoots another student in the arm with a small-caliber handgun as they argue between classes in a hallway at John Marshall High School.

OCT. 5–9: HOUSTON, TX. A gang fight among students at Northbrook High leaves sixteen-year-old Luis Mesa dead and another student in the hospital with shotgun wounds. The shootout took place on a nearby elementary school playground.

OCT. 12–16: HOUSTON, TX. Oscar Daniel Leon, a sixteen-year-old student at Desert View High School, is shot and killed with a .22-caliber pistol in the school parking lot.

OCT. 19–23: HOUSTON, TX. A ninth-grader at Barbara Jordan School for Careers is shot in the thigh with a .25-caliber pistol she says she found in a classmate's backpack.

OCT. 26–30: LITTLE ROCK, AR. Twelve students and their teacher at McClellan High School scramble for cover as gunshots shatter the glass door of their classroom. An eighteen-year-old and fifteen-year-old later are arrested.

NOV. 2–6: RICHARDSON, TX. Sean Patrick Cooper, a seventeen-year-old student at Berkner High School, is forced from his car near the parking lot after a Nov. 6 football game. He is then shot and killed. Eleven people, including students from a rival school, are arrested. (Tish Wells, "Week by Week, Guns Take a Toll in Schools," *USA Today*, 6A, Thursday, June 3, 1993.)

In order to understand *why* we have all the violence in America we must discern the "antecedents" for violence. When we realize that violence is a *force,* we begin to understand that it is a power to control, persuade, compel, take, and to injure. Violence is not natural! It is driven by antecedents of rhetoric, ideology, images, impressions, thoughts, and concepts.

In other words, when our kids see all the imagery of violence in media, movies, music, and our own homes, and hear all the negative rhetoric of some celebrities, they are motivated to violence. If you add to this motivation feelings of hopelessness or worthlessness, you are getting close to a violent act. All you need to complete the action is to have a catalyst of one of the negative emotions of fear, hatred, anger, hostility, bitterness, or rejection. Then, the stage is set for violence!

How can we stop this in our homes? We begin by maintaining order, peace, and love in our homes. There is no question that most violence begins in the home. It is either between the family members, or it is an incentive for the person to go outside of the home and commit a violent act.

Our house must become a synergistic home where all members are working together in a spirit of love, not where we use bargain chips to get or take what we want. The home should be where we share and care to the point where order prevails and any form of violence is out of order.

The beauty of our synergy as a family is that the prevailing attitude we have when we leave our home travels with us all day until we return. It motivates us to do acts of kindness toward others. If it is negative or destructive, however, it will motivate us to inflict destruction on others. It becomes a case of *pass it on.* Since I have it rough, I'll see to it that whoever I come in contact with will have it rough. Violence breeds violence. The opposite is also true. Love breeds love. It has always been that way. It will never change.

When we step outside of our home, we need other elements of society to promote order and harmony and not promote violence. Our kids need inspiration from celebrities and those who are in the limelight. We must regulate how much violence the entertainment media can exhibit and put before the faces of our kids.

We must evaluate what type of parenting role model we display for our kids. Tony, a seventeen-year-old young man, was regularly beating his girlfriend. He would punch her, knock her down, and threaten her. When Tony got the least bit jealous over his girlfriend, he would let her have it. She lived in mortal fear. Why would Tony behave like this? The girlfriend later confessed that Tony's dad beat his mother.

Violence in our kids can be traced to some of us as parents. If you explode in anger, venting your frustrations by some type of violent act against a family member, *expect* your children to do the same. When they commit a crime and injure or kill some innocent person, don't act dumbfounded as to why they did it. They are simply following your example.

Ruin/Violence Prevention Strategy

We can prevent the violence trend in our own homes and in our communities. Here's how:

1. We must never surrender to violence in any form in our home as acceptable behavior. Our homes must model a tranquil atmosphere of love and communication when conflict and disagreement occur.
2. We must take back our neighborhoods from any gang activity or violence promoters.
3. We must have a Community Network Plan to prevent violence before it occurs.
4. Our Network must include business, school, family, church, and government.

5. We must be proactive — preventing the crisis, not reactive — acting after the crisis has happened.
6. We must develop a tutoring and mentoring program to help high-risk kids of violence in our community or adjacent community.
7. We must challenge celebrities to "cool it" with their violent rhetoric and their actions.
8. We must monitor costly government programs that are only Band-Aids and are not realistic.
9. We must involve God, the church, prayer, and the Bible.
10. We must assist our schools, and not throw rocks from the sidelines.

Our example can change the behavior of our kids. When some other force interferes in our children's lives, we must be there to stop it.

$\cdot \ \cdot \ \cdot$

Chapter 15

$\cdot \ \cdot \ \cdot$

Teach Me How, Aunt Sara
Step #14 — Pray with Them!

I have met many parents who are in deep pain because of the problems with their children. Their kids are on their way to ruin, and they know it. Perhaps the most often-asked question these troubled parents pose to me is "What can we do, Jerry?" These parents are desperate and extremely concerned. Some of them are experiencing physical and emotional problems because of the upheaval in their homes.

The various steps outlined in this book tell parents what they can do. Some respond and say, "It is too late. I have already lost them." I know of one thing that can salvage even the worst kid in the worst circumstances — **prayer!** I could give story after story of young people who were bound for destruction, and a parent's prayer kept them out of a coffin.

. . .

*Prayer gives you courage to make
the decisions you must in crisis
and then the confidence to leave
the results to a Higher Power.
— President Dwight D. Eisenhower*

. . .

You must pray with your kids. If you don't know how, consider that prayer is talking to God as simply as you talk on the telephone to a friend. There is one word I focus on when I want to pray because I have read it several times in the Bible. It is the word "supplication." You seldom hear anyone today talking about how they supplicated. But what does this word mean?

What an important word! In fact, one verse offers an excellent description of it: "Don't worry about anything; instead, pray about everything; tell God your needs and don't forget to thank Him for His answers" (Phil. 4:6). Supplication means "tell God your needs, and don't forget to thank Him."

. . .

Seven days without prayer
makes one weak.
— The Bible Friend

. . .

Chances are there are probably needs in your home even while you are reading this book. You may be concerned about your son or daughter, the influence of their friends, or maybe your marriage. Problems are not terrible; they give God an opportunity to show us how strong He can work on our behalf. And we grow through our problems. They hurt for the time being. Nevertheless, we can come out of them stronger and better.

I Almost Died But...

I never met my grandmother on my dad's side of the family. My father has told me a lot about her. One thing Dad has made clear to me—she prayed all the time. She also prayed for her children's children. Her prayer was for God to raise them up to serve Him.

Grandma lived in Fort Scott, Kansas, in an extremely

modest home. In fact, she lived in virtual poverty. Her dresses were made out of the sacks that brought grain to little Fort Scott. She had nothing as far as this world was concerned. And yet, she was a mighty prayer warrior.

As a teenager, I almost died. I was doing drugs, had been hospitalized twice, and was checked out of St. Luke's Hospital weighing a grim sixty-eight pounds. My family was saturated with problems. When I came home from the hospital on Easter Sunday, my parents faced the possible, inevitable conclusion that I might not live to see sixteen years of age.

I believe my grandmother's prayers were working on my behalf without me even knowing it. A man across the street, Dave Wickersham, had watched the problems our family was experiencing. Dave approached my dad shortly after my arrival home and strongly urged him to send me to a youth camp with his church's youth group. I did not want to go. In my mind, Christians were either Boy Scouts or grandmas. I said to my dad, "No way!"

On May 12th, my birthday, Dad surprised me by buying me a professional football table. He said it was mine with one stipulation. He would take it back unless I went to camp. Since I did not want to lose my gift, I went very reluctantly the third week of June to camp.

What an experience! I had never been around people like these in all my life. One thing I noticed: These kids prayed. They prayed before breakfast, lunch, dinner, before the speaker, Bob Werner, and before we went to bed at night in our cabin.

I was used to a formal, almost handwritten prayer our freeze-dried minister uttered each Sunday morning in our cold church. This was different. There was something very real about these kids and their prayers.

Meanwhile, a vivacious girl by the name of Cindy Gibson had been praying for me all week. I had noticed her, especially her lovely, long, brown hair. She was stunning! Cindy knew all my past troubles and had started prayer cells for me all over camp. Cindy had even gone to Bob Werner and said, "Pray for Jerry Johnston." Many people throughout that camp were praying every day for me.

The last night, June 21st, I was in the back row of the camp auditorium at Windemere. Five minutes after the last meeting began, Cindy got up from her second row seat and headed straight for me in the back row. I saw her coming! I thought, *Great, maybe she will sit with me back here.*

"Jerry, I want you to come sit with me tonight," she said, as she reached out her hand and put it right in front of my face.

"Sure!" I exclaimed, jumping up and with great glee following one of the prettiest girls in the camp to my reserved, second-row seat. Bob Werner, the speaker, seemed like a giant towering above me from my vantage point. Had I not had the consolation of Cindy next to me, I would have fled to the back row.

That night Bob clearly explained that Jesus Christ died on the cross centuries ago to pay for my sins. He pointed out that people do not become Christians because they attend church or simply believe in God. Bob stated that just as we open the front door of our home and allow a visitor to come inside, so it is with Jesus when we experience the spiritual new birth. "You must invite Jesus Christ to come into your life if you want to go to heaven someday," Bob said.

As sensational as it sounds, it was as if that night the blinders that had been on my eyes suddenly dropped. I saw clearly that there is a God, and through the person of His Son Jesus Christ, He could change my life. I prayed my first prayer that night: "Jesus, I know I am lost. Thank You that You died for me. Come into my life right now. Make me a new person."

In a moment, my spiritual new birth occurred. I was on cloud nine and seemingly could not come back down to earth. After the meeting, I raced to find the camp speaker, Bob Werner. I poured out to Bob all the lurid things I had done before that week of camp. He listened and said, "Jerry,

God is going to use your life in a mighty way." I didn't know about that; I just knew for the first time in my life I felt great, actually happy and fulfilled. Bob later wrote a letter about his impressions of me at that camp—how he had prayed for me, along with all the others. Here is that letter:

The setting was Windemere Assembly, located on the Lake of the Ozarks in central Missouri. The emphasis for the week was Kansas City Youth Week, and I was invited to be the guest speaker. I always looked forward to these experiences because I had a deep love for the teenagers then and still do today. Some 700 kids filled the place, and the atmosphere was literally charged with spiritual electricity. I knew many of the kids did not know Christ, and another large group of kids were Christians and members of local churches, but their lives were inconsistent and their level of commitment was very shallow. I prayed that God would use me in some way to speak to those kids.

About Tuesday or Wednesday of that week, some of the kids told me about a young man who was with their youth group and was lost. They pointed him out to me. He was a small, very skinny young man with long, greasy hair. I remember he wore a pair of blue jeans with a marijuana patch sewed on the back pocket. There was something about him that really placed a burden on my heart for his salvation. I would see him on the campus during the day, usually alone, not taking part in the activities. I noticed that during the services at night he would sit in the back where most of the kids talk. So I was sure he was not getting much out of what was being said. We had one last big evangelistic service planned for Thursday night, and I knew it was going to be my last chance to reach him. One very beautiful young Christian girl invited him to sit with them up in front. That night, when I began to preach, I saw Jerry sitting there on the third row, and I knew this was going to be the night. I presented the plan of salvation as clearly as I could, and when I gave the invitation, dozens and dozens of kids responded. Jerry was one of them. I remember meeting him down in front of the auditorium, putting my arms around him and hugging him, and asking him if he was coming to give his life to Christ. He said yes and went off to the counseling area.

The next morning, he was extremely happy about the decision he had made, and I could see a change in his face. In the weeks that followed, he corresponded with me. I promised to send him a Living Bible, which I did, and he read it, rather consumed it in his new beginning with God. Not many months after his conversion, he indicated in a letter that he felt maybe God was calling him to preach. I have to admit, I thought that it was a premature response from an overzealous convert, but nonetheless, I encouraged him. He asked if I had any books with sermons in them, and I responded by sending him one of Herschel Ford's simple sermon books. A month or so later, he wrote again asking if I had any more of those books. So I sent him another one. I think I sent a total of five or six over a period of several months. I found out later that Jerry was taking these simple sermons and putting them into his own words and preaching them at every opportunity he had.

Some years later, I saw Dr. Jerry Falwell at a meeting of ministers in Washington, D.C. I identified myself by telling him that I was the pastor who was preaching the night Jerry Johnston was saved, and his comment was "You caught a big fish that time, didn't you."

I've looked back on that moment many times, and I never cease to marvel at the grace of God. Who would have believed that little, skinny, greasy-haired teenager would become God's spokesman and used so powerfully to impact the lives of so many across the country today. I'll always thank God that He let me be there to see it happen.

When I came home from camp and told my parents about my newfound faith, they were dumbfounded, but very happy. Through the years, they encouraged everything God was doing in my life. My dad became quite close to me and has been my mentor in many areas.

The first two months after I arrived home from camp, my former drug friends circulated throughout the community saying, "Jerry is a narc. Get him." It wasn't true. I didn't narc on anyone; my supposed friends were ready to try to injure or hurt me.

My dad sent me to live with my Aunt Sara. She had a flower shop—the best in Kansas City. For two months, my aunt and Uncle Don disciplined me, loved me, taught me, and treated me as if I was their own son. It was those two vital months that put cement and longevity into the spiritual commitment I had made.

My Aunt Sara taught me by her example how to pray. I would work in the flower shop cleaning and sweeping the floor. When we closed the shop, we would leave on deliveries. Up one street and down another, Aunt Sara would teach me about faith, how to know God, and, most importantly, how to pray.

When we finally arrived at her home, we would eat a very late dinner. At the end of a long day, Aunt Sara would take me out into her beautiful living room with the red carpet in the front of her house. We would get down on our knees and pray. These were no "God, bless-the-world-let's-hurry-up-and-go-to-bed prayers." Aunt Sara would pray quite a long time. When she stopped, it was my turn. I learned to pray by listening to her. She taught me how to pray by her example.

During these two important months, I was grounded in my faith. I learned that my walk with God was not a Sunday-morning-for-two-hours type of thing. I learned it was, as Aunt Sara said repeatedly, "a moment-by-moment walk."

As a parent, I pray daily with my children. When one of them comes home from school disturbed by some problem, we pray. We try to pray collectively as a family each day. Sometimes the schedule interrupts, and we know when we have gone too long without our united time together in prayer.

. . .

Some parents are funny. They refuse
to give a child the keys to the car

> *because they feel he is not mature enough*
> *to make the proper decisions*
> *imperative to safe driving. Yet, they*
> *refuse to direct the religious life*
> *of the child because they say he should*
> *arrive at his own conclusions.*
> — *F.D. Elliot*

. . .

How do families who do not pray endure their problems? I will never know. Perhaps that is why we have a divorce rate in America of one out of every two marriages.

Learn to pray with your kids on a daily basis. Pray about everything. When you are indecisive about what job you should take, what decision you should make, who they should date, what career choice they should choose, **PRAY WITH THEM!** Watch God work on your behalf. You will record memories and victories together that you will savor the rest of your lives.

The most important prayer parents pray with their son or daughter is the prayer for them to invite Jesus Christ to come into his or her life. Are your children Christians? Do they really *know* Christ? Is their faith vital? Is it real? Is it a day-by-day growing experience? Maybe they are as spiritual as you are.

There have been times when I had to tell Danielle, Jeremy, and Jenilee, "I'm sorry. I've been a poor example. Please forgive me." I learned kids are very forgiving if we are honest.

There has been no greater thrill in my life than leading my children to Jesus Christ. Danielle came to Christ in Chattanooga; Jeremy in Dallas; and Jenilee in Wichita. I had the honor to pray with each one of them the moment they were born again in God's eternal family. Those are very distinct memories with each one of them.

. . .

*To the thousands of students who
wrote to poet Carl Sandburg, asking
him how to become a writer, Sandburg
replied, "Solitude and prayer —
then go from there."*

. . .

You might want to close this book by rededicating your life to God. Ask the Lord to take over in your life, your spouse's life, and your family. Watch Him work miracles. He has the answers to your problems. He is just waiting for you to give it all to Him. Tell your kids of your new commitment. They might be skeptical. That's OK. Simply allow your light to starting shining. It will penetrate any darkness in your home.

If you have a story you want to tell, write me. If I can help your family like God has helped mine, let me hear from you.

Jerry Johnston
P.O. Box 12193
Overland Park, KS 66282-2193

Recommended Reading

Here are books I recommend every parent to read. They are prized possessions in my personal library at home.

Barna, George. *The Future of the American Family.* Chicago: Moody Press.

Bennett, William J. *The De-valuing of America: The Fight for Our Culture and Our Children.* New York: A Touchstone Book.

Dobson, James, and Gary L. Bauer. *Children at Risk.* Dallas: Word Publishers, 1990.

Eyre, Linda and Richard. *Teaching Your Children Values.* New York: Simon and Schuster.

Forbes, Malcolm, with Jeff Bloch. *What Happened to Their Kids?* New York: Simon and Schuster, 1990.

Go Ask Alice. New York: Avon Books, 1971.

Halberstam, David. *The Fifties.* New York: Villard Books.

Hayes, E. Kent. *Why Good Parents Have Bad Kids.* New York: Doubleday Dell Publishing Group, 1991.

Medved, Michael. *Hollywood vs. America.* New York: Harper Collins Books.

Olson, G. Keith. *Counseling Teenagers.* Loveland, Colo.: Group Books, 1984.

Rice. John R. *The Home.* Murfreesboro, Tenn.: Sword of the Lord Publishers.

Schulman, Michael, and Eva Mekler. *Bringing Up a Moral Child.* New York: Doubleday Dell Publishing Group, 1985.

Sparks, Beatrice. *Jay's Journal.* New York: A Dell Book, 1989.

Spotts, Dwight, and David Veerman. *Reaching Out to Troubled Youth.* Wheaton, Ill.: Victor Books, 1987.

Stanley, Charles. *How to Keep Your Kids on Your Team.* Nashville: Oliver Nelson Books, 1986.